ACCLIM

A Personal and Reflective Approach
to a Natural Relationship

by
Steve Van Matre

Published by the American Camping Association
Bradford Woods
Martinsville, Indiana 46151

Cover Photo Courtesy of
Kimberly Clark Paper Co., Inc.

International Standard Book Number:
0-87603-016-9

Printed in the United States of America

Dedicated

to

"the group"

JIM WELLS

HARRY HOOGESTEGER

PAT WALKUP

DONN EDWARDS

ACKNOWLEDGEMENTS

I used to think that acknowledgements were rather absurd. But then, I once held to the conviction that committees could not write books! Both are untrue. For ACCLIMATIZING, like its predecessor ACCLIMATIZATION, is the product of a concerted group effort. Now, how does one go about properly thanking a committee?

Let's start with a low bow to "the group" that got it all together:

Jim Wells
Pat Walkup
Harry Hoogesteger
Donn Edwards

then a tip of the hat to the photographic helpers:

Doug Kittredge   Bruce Barnett

and the typists:

Pat Arndt   Ellen Goldberg

Let's conclude with special thanks to special assistants:

John Caviale   Dave Howe

a separate acknowledgement for separate sharing:

Oliver Gillespie   Stan Lock

(Stan for the idea of WHEELS; Oliver for LASSOING AN ANT and the CAMOUFLAGE GAME)

and a salute to:

John Jordan and
Towering Pines where it all happened,
Nelson Wieters and
George Williams College where it was all edited,
Eleanor Eells and the
Fund for Advancement of Camping who made it all possible.

"Acclimatization was like six hours of preparation before playing the game.

Acclimatizing IS the game!"

TABLE OF CONTENTS

ACCLIMATIZING IS . . .

AN INTRODUCTION

"Start where the learner is, not where you are," reads one of our axioms for leaders. And as a result, I find myself in something of a predicament for I feel some inner pressure to tell you where I am coming from nonetheless. Perhaps I have been reading too much Perls (as one of my favorite professors was once wont to put it, "Steve, you've been reading too many damn books again!"), for I believe I must be "up front" with you about some of my more relevant thoughts and feelings. At any rate, it would be impossible for me to know where all of you are. This way, if by chance you can get your head into grasping (not agreeing with) my viewpoint, we'll both be starting from somewhere a little closer -- which is far more than most introductions do for you anyway. So let's begin with a look at where I am.

I.

I CANNOT PRETEND TO BE AN EXPERT IN ENVIRONMENTAL EDUCATION.

In fact, I cannot even pretend to know what it is. I suspect that it is merely good education in general (which means we might be more appropriately classified as lobbyists instead of educators). From listening to others, environmental education would appear to be a process applicable to most any content. Unlike the serious academic discipline, there seems to be no recognizable body of knowledge. (There are evidently no standard skills either -- unless plaster casting or measuring air pollution will pass for requisite abilities.)

In the beginning, "outdoor education" may have been a more telling title, but the term indicates for me how far we've departed from our natural origins. It is only from the entrenched mental position of someone who spends a great deal of time "inside" doors, shut off from growing things and raw nutrients, that one could speak of the "outdoors." To use the term "outdoor education" continually hints at the strange paradox within which we find ourselves.

Enough. I don't want to quibble needlessly, for it is good to take youngsters outside of those damn buildings for whatever reason. Let's just say that I am interested in education for living as part of the natural world (that natural world which exists in spite of man's present aberrations), and that I am engaged in helping young people learn about themselves, not as isolated entities, but each one as a coalescence in the sun's web of life.

I BELIEVE NATURAL RESOURCES ARE NOT THINGS, BUT COMMUNITIES.

It is not the lumber, but the forest which represents the true natural resource. If we could but change an entire nation's concept of resources, we might change our self-consumptive approach to this rather magnificent yet imperilled sunship.

Let's begin by burning all of those old grade school lists of natural resources. They splinter both the enumeration and the enterprise. Man's natural resources are not individual things, but whole communities, even though their components may resemble the resources of yesteryear.

The American Indian was correct in his characterization of "mother earth." Intuitively perhaps, the Indian realized that one cannot destroy the giver in the process of sharing the gifts. It's the ubiquitous goose of the fables. The forest community may provide a certain amount of coal, or lumber, or natural water storage, or a hundred-hundred other commodities, but man can only take so much before endangering the source of that supply itself. (How simple the conclusion; how imperceptive the players.) To allow the incessant destruction of these communities is to destroy the taproot of our existence. Any time that you hear of someone clear-cutting a forest, or strip mining a mountain, or draining a marsh, or paving a meadow you should scream rape from the nearest rooftop. Yes, I know, if my advice were to be followed, we would have one-half of the populace tearing up the land and the other half recklessly running around shouting "rape." But is there another way?

III.

I AM CONCERNED ABOUT ESSENTIAL CONCEPTS OF ECOLOGY.

Make no mistake, there is a malaise upon the land. The film of life glazing planet earth has given birth to a parasitic species of intense destructive capabilities. It seems that man may well perform the heretofore ecologically unthinkable act: either to consume his own community -- or so foul his own quarters as to make living there untenable. In Longfellow's words "whom the Gods would destroy they first make mad." And at the moment, it would appear that man has taken gigantic steps toward that destiny.

Is there any hope for reversing this onslaught in the future? That's a question which may best be answered by asking another: do our young people know what a habitat is -- or a cycle -- or a community? And not because they have seen a picture of one, but because they are aware that they have been in touch with its actual components? Since they are inextricably bound up with all three of these, how extraordinarily sad it is that we should insist upon their ability to conceptualize a mathematical equation, yet not a forest community. Further, I dare suggest that measuring water pollution is not as momentous as grasping the concept of the water CYCLE. Without the latter, the former is merely an interesting exercise in contemporary affairs rather than a building block of enduring awareness. And with a nod to the vernacular of those who espouse "basic" education, great effort is expended to make sure our miniature scholars can accurately sort metallic discs, a task to which they have learned to attach the special significance called "making change," but they remain strangely mute when asked to explain the interdependence of life. In fairness to these youngster's innate capacities IT IS difficult to attach much feeling to an unexperienced pictorial representation, or a teacher's abstract description. Not so if you have been there -- if you have followed a raindrop, role-played a frog, or lived in a woodchuck's den!

It is almost beyond belief. We know so little about how people learn, then set about methodically ignoring most of what we do know. In fact, much of education today still relies upon the fervent hope that the means will so condition the ends that eventually youngsters will arrive with neat little funnels already screwed into their craniums. A great number of teachers continue to dedicate their lives to setting up environmental conditions which serve this goal. They begin by positing questions for which they already have answers, and end by reciting answers themselves to questions no one asked. In the other direction, you now have a great number of those who chant the advantages of a "do your own thing" curriculum, but all too many of these neo-pedagogues seem to end up by denying their own thing, or making a thing of denial. Either of these two extremes is surely destined to enervate the brain cells of even the most energetic youngsters (while keeping those little posteriors glued to fixed seats). Little wonder then that we continue to have such difficulty in turning out ecologically experienced adults.

IV.

I REMAIN CONVINCED THAT WHERE IT'S AT IS IN THE WHOLENESS OF OUR THRUST.

Mind. Body. Not two, but one. Interlink: mind/body. The total organism must grapple with the experience. It's learning by good doing, and good doing is multi-sensory.

First, we must deal with the whole person. Get behind the words. As you are reading this, stop for a moment and just listen. . . . Chances are good that a little voice in the attic of your mind was naming the sounds around you. *But the sounds are not their names.* The sound is not "fan," but something like "whirrrrr. . ." You see, each of us serves as the home for a tiny, yet persistent voice in our head. Surprisingly, that mental gossip has the capacity to both illuminate AND insulate. Uncontrolled, it can turn us into walking corpses. (A fate which we appear to pursue with some diligence as we continue to favor intellectualizers in place of intellectuals; verbalize, but do not feel; think instead of doing; become anesthetized rather than sensitized to our surroundings; and isolate ourselves from our natural origins!)

Second, we must strive to merge with the environment, not overcome it. To pit your energies against nature is to do battle with yourself. And you can neither conquer the mountain, nor your own body. You are what you are. You may be able to do more than you thought you could, but it is an illusion to think that you can rise above yourself.

The so-called "tripping" program, which has long held a preeminent position in the camping movement, should be a ready-made vehicle for conscious and considered mind/body involvement in the natural world. It is strangely unfortunate then that so many of these "vehicles" continue to perpetuate the idea of a physical struggle as the major thrust of their activity. That approach too often fosters an artificial detachment, an unhealthy duality: mind OVER body and mind OVER nature. It is our intention to promote unifying experiences. In our program, traditional campcraft activities, survival training, and physical ordeals are relegated to an adjunct level at best. Our format emphasizes individual awareness and sensitivity. Our interest lies in maximizing time for natural observation and personal expression. Our goal is not to cover distance, but uncover feelings. Our thrust is not to contrive forced situations based upon a stress philosophy, but to instill a natural openness for unitive and reflective growth -- "a heart that watches and receives."

I AM INTERESTED IN FOSTERING INDIVIDUAL GROWTH AND DEVELOPMENT.

In an era of group *sub*mersion ACC emphasizes individual *im*mersion. It is not so much how one gets along with others, but how one gets along with oneself. We believe accepting yourself is more important than others accepting you.

Lest we forget, the nature of life is nature. (All of man's projections notwithstanding.) Bodies grow. They need light and air and water and soil just like the tree outside your window. And, like plants, bodies thrive with space and attention; they need to learn to move with the wind and endure the stillness. *The key to healthy growth is individual awareness.* Young people need room to roam and freedom to explore. It is vital that we nourish the integrity of the young person, not constrain or contract him by stuffing him into a role or a norm too small for his individuality. Getting along with others usually happens naturally when a youngster has a high degree of *self*-acceptance.

Through special techniques ACCLIMATIZING permeates the barriers which resist awareness, and strengthens the motivators which encourage. Where ACCLIMATIZATION is designed to introduce all newcomers to their natural environment, *Acclimatizing* personalizes the experience. *Acclimatization was like six hours of preparation before playing the game. Acclimatizing IS the game!* ACCLIMATIZATION breaks down the initial barriers and provides receiving "frames" for ecological understanding. *Acclimatizing* not only goes beyond those primary barriers and conceptual frames, but also undertakes a life-long approach to a personal way of relating with the natural world.

VI.

I FEEL THAT SELF-AWARENESS FOLLOWS NATURAL AWARENESS, and that it is most often a by-product of pursuing the latter rather than the result of being sought after as an end in itself.

There has been and continues to be too much emphasis upon striving for self-awareness. It will probably not come like a thunderbolt but a tingle. It is not found by active seeking. Self-awareness comes not so much from talking as from listening: illuminate the self by not focusing on the self.

Regardless of how much effort -- how many groups joined, how many costume changes, how many things one gets "into" -- self-awareness will most likely come at the precise moment when it is not being sought. And it is likely to sneak up when one's back is bent in simple work. It must not be looked for within, but without.

Neither can one sit and wait for it, one must go about the art of living. For above all, it will come to those who are growing. Feel within. Think without.

The path to self-awareness is the road home.

VII.

I AM TAKEN UP WITH BEAUTY.

On the threshold of the age of plasticity I know this sounds strange, but we find beauty in natural objects. It is important for a young person to see the exquisite lines, the interrelatedness, the formidability yet fragility of all life; to see the pattern, the delicate harmony, and the balance of all living things. Francis Thompson said it with poetic grace "Thou canst not stir a flower without troubling of a star."

ACC is living poetry. It deals with the rhythms of life itself. And poetry is the tongue of magic. Whatever else we do we hope to instill a spirit of *joie de vivre.* We aim to create a breathless sense of excitement, and wonder, and love for life. Our fabric is spun from a varied spectrum of natural but joyous activities. And our stimulus is not always "loud," or "heavy," or "bright." There is as much room for a whisper as a shout. Above all, it need not be synthetic.

The Japanese have a word for a quality that transcends beauty. They call it "shibui." Objects possessing "shibui" have great beauty, but they are also natural, simple, commonplace, humble, quiet, imperfect, and free. Preeminently perhaps, they exhibit a deep inner meaning. In many respects, that's what ACC is all about. Acclimatizing is living beautifully.

VIII.

IN THE END, I DEAL IN MAGIC, BUT HAVE NO MAGIC POTION.

The ACC books are no substitute for work. Unfortunately, this is something you have to do in order for it to be successful. I cannot provide the sweat for your setting and schedule. However, I do have some tips left.

A word of warning: GOOD TEACHERS DO NOT TEACH; THEY CREATE EXCITING LEARNING SITUATIONS. That's the real chore. You must first decide what it is that you want to help someone learn (another one of those "seldom-done" even though obvious postulates of education). Next, you must create a learning situation -- a DOING situation -- involving as many senses as possible. Finally, you must ask yourself: "Is this fun?" No, all learning need not be a lark. But then, neither should it be drudgery. Another often overlooked common sense item is that we seem to learn best what we enjoy most. Did you ever notice though, it's almost always those who have trouble figuring out anything very exciting that first suggest that everything shouldn't be? For me, I like fun, and I don't feel even the slightest pang of guilt in saying so. Let's make learning a good thing again.

Remember: concepts are not built in a day. It takes time. A little girl may call a moth a bird -- she possibly hasn't distinguished between various kinds of moving things with wings -- but the parameters of her conceptual frame will change as she accumulates new data. So it is with the concept of a habitat -- or a cycle -- or a community. At best, each activity you set up is a concept BUILDER. Lots of these building segments (strung together like the links of a chain) will eventually result in a fair grasp of the concept. Stick to it.

Stay on target: use cryptic phrases to trigger more appropriate responses. (Yes, as you have guessed, I am something of a compulsive aphorist.) A good way to utilize what you read is to sum it up in a line. Do not hesitate to borrow from or paraphrase others:

"Everything goes somewhere" (Barry Commoner).

"You can't do just one thing" (Garrett Hardin).

"Do more with less" (John Holt).

And when in doubt, use some of ours:

"When you care, they care."

"Don't react, respond."

"Everything has a home."

OK. So now you have some idea of where I've been since penning the introduction to *Acclimatization*. When I and my ACC cohorts undertook that project, we were trying to provide a short, introductory program to use with all newcomers to the camp setting. Now we're trying to answer the question, "so we've run everyone through *Acclimatization*, what's next?" Some of our answers can be found in the following pages, others have yet to be refined. You can help. Drop us a line about your discoveries. We're insatiable.

S.V.M.
Associate Director
Towering Pines
August, 1973

NATURAL AWARENESS

I know this place too well--but do I really? Maybe if I look at it from a different angle, change my whole perspective, then it will be new. Will that happen?

I saw a little red, a tiny little red spider, crawling over the white sand, and it was really amazing watching that tiny little thing crawling over those huge boulders. Kind of strange, but it must be awfully different when you're that size.

Something about this whole time, place, and feeling keeps me mystified about life itself. "Why was I put here on earth?" I asked my pine cone, and he said: "To search, seek, grab life, happiness, and insight by the handful, and to share it."

The word "aware" comes from an Old English root meaning to be watchful, or on the alert.

ALERT! That word still conveys the urgency of the moment; the immediacy of bringing one's entire self to bear; to be ready, with all senses operating at peak efficiency, on the very edge of action. Alertness is those tension-building seconds as the coiled spring of the body tightens itself.

Being fully aware has something of that same sharpness of emotion; a crisp, tingling clarity of perception. It is keeping all senses fully functioning. Being aware is like having a head-start on alertness. The whole being is in a state of relaxed action. Awareness is this ongoing wholeness. It is a knowing growth.

"Natural" awareness is a many-sided quality: it is an illuminating beacon stabbing through a foggy understanding of life; it is the ability to feel unseen dimensions of the non-human world; and not least, it is ongoing therapy for the affectively retarded! Natural awareness is THAT -- the natural world. Acclimatizing is US IN THAT. And it is a synergistic us.

William Blake said, "If the doors of perception could be cleansed, all things would be seen as they are, infinite." The world is here in all its splendor. We need only to "clean our doors" a bit and allow a free flow from the world to enter us. And in turn, with undisturbed perception, we can enter a world as potentially rich as the whole of human heritage, where the familiar becomes the unfamiliar, the ordinary the miraculous.

A small child enters totally into that world. There is no inner and outer dimension. There is no analysis or consciousness of time or withholding of self. What there is in the child's mind is the joy of play and the total giving of self to the moment.

It is possible, if we take the path seriously, to pursue awareness until we return to that childlike innocence and harmony -- only on a "higher" level. With all the faculties of an adult we can still be our spontaneous selves, entering freely, uninhibitedly, the rich perceptual worlds around us. It isn't easy -- and it's a lifetime task, perhaps -- but it is immensely rewarding.

Here are three developmental rules to follow:

I. YOU ARE NOT YOUR HEAD

Many people view their body as something for their head to ride around on. Watch for them. They are everywhere.

For hundreds of thousands of years nature has been bringing forth life in beautiful, varied, and increasingly complex manifestations. You are a highly tuned organism standing at the present pinnacle of that development -- a terribly complex animal of quite unbelievable capacities.

You are a piece of the sun.

You are not a worm with a swollen sensory appendage on one end. Wiggle your toes. Every waking hour you should do that -- just to make sure you keep both ends in focus! And I don't mean just knowing it's there. It's more than that -- it's knowing that it's YOU. You are your foot!

You must "beware" of following where your head leads. The trick is not to become addicted to your own inner voice. Don't take it too seriously. Every day you do more that you DON'T consciously think about than you do that you do consciously think about -- and you always will! You -- your whole body -- are doing a thousand-thousand "unthought" things just while reading this page.

When people say they shake their head to clear it, they simply mean that they loosen the grasp which their mental voice has affixed them with. Remember: this voice deals in abstractions. Its words are not the things themselves. And its home in the attic of your mind is cluttered with the junk of your past. Don't let the abstractions and the memories get between you and your toes!

Lao-tsu said it: "Learning consists in adding to one's stock day by day. The practice of the Tao consists in subtracting." Clean out your attic.

II. LISTEN TO NATURAL VOICES

After warning you about the pitfalls of listening to yourself talk, let me encourage you to listen to your feelings. Listen to your whole body.

Have you ever taken one minute, or even thirty seconds, stopped and DONE NOTHING except listen to yourself breathe? Try it. It is immediately calming and relaxing; sometimes you can feel your heart pumping away within your chest, sometimes you are just aware of the air coming in and going out in its mysteriously refreshing way. The breathing is involuntary and rhythmic -- like waves rolling in from the ocean. It is very peaceful.

In listening to natural voices the idea is to NOT concentrate. Relax. Let thoughts flow THROUGH you. In contemplation the self is passive in relation to its subject. Let your inner mechanisms operate without your ego getting in the way. Man may well be doomed as a viable species unless he can reawaken his natural voices and his capacity to genuinely listen to the voices of nature. So get out of your own light and your own voice!

You listen to natural voices by not listening to yourself. Sound confusing? It's actually simple. Ordinarily, when you listen, you pay attention. The idea here is that you just don't pay attention to your MENTAL voice. When certainty of thought comes, it arrives as a surge of feeling not as a deluge of words.

EVERYTHING has its own sound. Go sit on a rock and listen.

III. GO OUTSIDE

Urban life militates against natural awareness. There are just too many obstacles, too many man-created barriers to overcome in the city. Surrounded by the accoutrements of an urban existence the chances of receiving a genuine message from the natural world are slim. The continual shriek and clatter, the chemical dust and artificial light bombard our sensory apparatus. We have not been pre-adapted for the pungent and corrosive synthetics of a city atmosphere. To experience nature as it is, we must shuck off the clamor of the modern city. And in the country, we must escape the confines of those same plasticized, stainless, permanenitized, streamlined dwellings. Literally, get out of the nest. Of all the planet's animals man seems to have an ever-lengthening nest life. Perhaps we are evolving into a species similar to those subterranean insect queens -- only we have created mechanical attendants for our feeding and grooming.

A SENSEless person in our language is either a) unintelligent or b) unconscious. On the other hand, look at two different words derived from sense: SENSible and SENSitive, both complementary. Our language, surprisingly, still holds the truth that to be aware of one's senses -- to perceive the world fully -- well, it makes good SENSE. And to perceive you must make contact. To be out "there." To get around those things which get between you and natural forces -- both mentally and physically.

The series of exercises which follow have been developed to aid one in capturing that illusive ability of being fully aware. The series is broken down into four stages: sharpening senses, seeking patterns, perceiving wholes, and distilling essence. The beginner would be well-advised to start with the initial exercises and work forward. If you do move around, sampling first one, then another, it is most important that you keep in touch with where you are (both what the exercise builds ON and what it is building TO).

Each exercise follows a pattern which may not be immediately apparent. There is an overall guideline followed by: something you do to set the stage, specific instructions for the exercise, an explanation for why you are doing it, and either something to think about or additional tasks.

A word of caution: the interesting thing about awareness is that our senses only give joy if we let them. "If we don't feel good, we can't do good." So if you feel either inattentive or just plain lousy today, please consider finding something else with which to occupy your time!

Before beginning, you should take up a comfortable position outside, or at least next to a window. Most of the exercises are enhanced by exposure. However, as many are applicable to a room as well as a retreat, you need not hesitate merely because you are presently in the middle of a city or engulfed by a snowstorm. In either case, try to get outside if only for a short walk. You must make some direct contact with natural forces. True awareness comes in small pieces.

Combinations, variations, and modifications of these eighteen exercises make up much of the remainder of the book. Overall the tasks are simple, short, and direct, but you will be amazed at how "new" they will become with the trying.

Altogether these exercises form our keyboard of perception. By running through these "keys" successively and with a little verve you can reach a crescendo of emotion, or by carefully building and prolonging you can achieve a feeling of oneness unmatched by other experiences.

Try a simple playing -- hitting just a few keys in the course of an afternoon -- or take several days and work your way leisurely through all four stages. Whichever approach you choose, this keyboard will aid your quest in becoming supremely tuned to the rhythms of the cosmos.

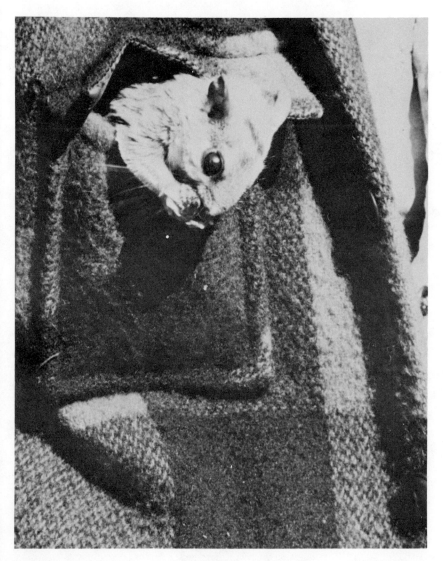

TOUCHING

TOUCH WITH YOUR HAND, BUT FEEL WITH YOUR BODY.

Pick up a natural object.
Close your eyes and use the palm of your hand to brush it lightly. Now rub the object along the skin on the inside of your arm. Pat it on your cheek. Take off your shoe and explore it with your bare sole.

Seven layers of skin make up your body's largest organ. It has many sensitive areas which can be used for touching. In order to heighten this sense you need only to experiment with your whole body.

Briskly and rapidly clap your hands together.
Stretch your fingers as you do so. Now touch things around you. Touch yourself.

Energy flows through your hands. Clapping sensitizes your receptors and heightens your flow of energy. HOW YOU TOUCH IS HOW YOU FEEL. Your hand is a sense receiving-gathering appendage. You can use it for more than a mechanical extension of your eyes.

Find a tree.
Caress, then massage its trunk. Now try this on a tree with another kind of bark. Use your nose, too.

This action places your whole hand in contact with the object and provides a good example of a multi-sensory way of comparing different things!

Think: how does the object feel that is being touched by me?

TASTING

EAT WITH ALL OF YOUR SENSES.
Select a piece of fruit.
Take a bite-sized piece first. Chew it slowly. As you do, start with a simple characterization of its taste, then begin reaching for a more precise description. Take another small piece. LIQUEFY, then swallow.

Our taste receptors can only distinguish four primary qualities: salty, sweet, bitter, and sour, but there are thousands of subtle blendings in between. By chewing until you have complete disintegration, you can savor the full range of taste.

Find something that you have not eaten recently.

Examine the item. Move it around in front of your eyes to catch different angles and various shadings of light. Now close your eyes and brush it with your lips and nose. Inhale its fragrance. Absorb its texture. Nibble. DON'T EAT, ASSIMILATE.

Taste is so obviously multi-sensory. Color and texture and smell play an important role in how we taste. Like everything else taste is heightened by preparation and anticipation.

Go play with your food!

HEARING

LISTEN TO THE PURITY OF SOUNDS.

Tap around your ears.
Relax. Breathe deeply. Close your eyes. Silence yourself. Listen.
Don't label the sounds, just experience them.
Without thoughts, without judging or comparing or naming, just listen. If you find difficulty in pure absorption, then attach letters which describe the sound. Is it the "rraawurrghh" of a motor, or the "whhhooossaaaa" of wind among leaves?
NAMES ARE NOT SOUNDS. If you want to talk about a sound, then a name may do, but if you want to HEAR it, then a name only gets in the way.
Sit back and just let the sounds penetrate your whole body.
Float with the sounds. Let the sounds move you. Inhale slowly and let your body vibrate in time with the sounds coming to it.
Your ears are funnels which gather and amplify the reverberations of sounds from the air, but your entire body soaks up those same waves. Sound affects all of you.
Tune in to the natural channels.

SMELLING

TRACE THE SMELLS AROUND YOU.

Breathe deeply.
Expand your nostrils. Suck the air up into the top of your nose. Don't sniff yet. INHALE AND HOLD. Now, sniff a little more up inside your nasal passages. Try to distinguish predominate odors, then follow them to their sources.

We are smelling all the time and don't know it. By breathing deeply we can bring more of the odors into contact with our olfactories. By following smells we can prolong our sensory sharpness.

Hold things up to your nose so you can pull the air in through them.

Moisten things before you smell them. Crumble or crush things in your hand. Rub plant juices on your body. Touch more with your nose. Follow the rain. Walk in the weeds!

Ask yourself how different scenes smell.

Don't just focus on how individual things smell. How does a room smell? -- a field? -- a sunset? How do you smell?

SEEING

CHANNEL OTHER SENSES THROUGH YOUR EYES.

Look up.

How would you describe the sky? Work at being precise in your visual account.

The sky is not blue. It may be robin's-egg, hyacinth, azure, or steel just for openers. There are an estimated seven million colors!

Feel the sky.

After pinning down its color, what about its texture, or smell, or taste? Is it heavy, smoky, or murky? How does it make YOU feel?

SEEING IS NOT RECEIVING. It is gathering light images and interpreting them on the basis of past receptions. We see as we have seen! To change our perception we must change our past. That's why it helps to vary our approach.

Look at something nearby.

Ask yourself: what was it like yesterday? What will happen to it tomorrow? Why is it called what it is? If it could speak, what would it say? How does it look from a different angle? How does it smell?

FEELING

PAY ATTENTION TO YOUR FEELINGS.

How do you feel?

No, not what do you think, but what do you FEEL? Overall, how does your body feel? Right now. Be specific.

Part of your natural voices are these non-verbal communications from your body. Many people use their body merely as a vehicle for their head. Not so. YOU ARE YOUR BODY.

Trace a feeling.

Where does it begin? Practice staying with it.

Don't turn it off. Don't suppress it. Flow with the feeling.

All senses are "feeling" senses. We literally FEEL the world with our different sensory probes. An "integrated" body is one in which all of the senses flow together. They have achieved a balance as each contributes to an overall harmony.

Prolong a feeling.

Start with a good, joyous feeling and keep it going. Don't let it fade. Hold on. Push it a little. Go beyond ecstasy.

FOCUSING

CONCENTRATE ON GATHERING MANY CLEAR IMAGES.

Close one eye and focus on the tip of your nose. Open your eye and shift your vision to something about two feet in front of you, now click your eyes into focus on an object four feet away -- now thirty feet away -- then one hundred feet -- two hundred -- finally, focus on the far horizon. Run through this same sequence two or three times. Note the feeling in your eyes.

Your eyes are superb binoculars. If you use them consciously, you can add visual layers to a scene. You can gain dimensions in feeling as well as seeing.

Let your eyes wander over the landscape.

Try to keep them moving at first. Sweep back and forth over the entire scene without stopping. Take your time. Now, pause on the USUAL. Focus on objects at various distances and angles. Look away, then return to focus again.

Search for designs in what you see.

Look for circles or spirals or cylinders or cones. Center your attention on an arrangement that is repeated. NOTE SPACING. Expand your focus to look for the distribution of like objects.

FRAMING

ENCLOSE SCENES WHICH YOU WANT TO EXAMINE.

Join your fists together to make a tubular "frame."
Look through your fists to frame objects near by. Try ONE leaf or ONE pebble or ONE pine cone.
Objects set off by themselves take on new depth. TO CENTER IS TO KNOW.
Make a square "frame" using the index finger and thumb of each hand.
Begin by finding objects around you which literally "fill" your frame. Try a section of the ground, or a stump, or a tree trunk. Now hold your frame closer to your eye and search out scenes on the horizon.
Analysis is aided by enclosure. Establishing boundaries briefly narrows perception and sharpens patterns.
Blink to "frame" with your eyelids.
Close your eyes, then blink rapidly a few times as you pan your eyes slowly across the landscape.
We see best when we don't try! By blinking rapidly we can gain impressions undimmed by our recollections or verbalizations. Relationships emerge naturally. Key features stand out plainly.

GROUPING

LOOK FOR ARRANGEMENTS IN FORMS AND LINES.

Find a comfortable spot with a good view.

Pull back mentally from the vista before you. Look at your scene as if it was a painted canvas. Just enjoy this picture. Note lighting and shadow and texture. Where does the picture itself carry your eye?

For this exercise you need some visual detachment: "you can't see the forest for the trees!" Lighting and color and texture and movement help set off the major elements of the composition before you.

Using your hand, block out the major groupings in your picture.

Outline them in space. Use quick, broad hand movements to represent the major elements of the scene before you. SQUINT your eyes to better see basic lines. Widen your eyes to better capture large groups.

The placement of primary shapes reveals the underlying unity of your scene. It clarifies what holds the scene together.

Finally, look at your scene as if from a mountain top. DRINK UP THE SCENE WITH YOUR EYES.

There are some pieces of beauty we want to remember.

EXPANDING

OBSERVE THE OVERALL ASPECTS OF A SCENE.

Look at the scene before you.

Try to approach the scene as if you've never seen it before. Note the way the light strikes various objects. SEEK OUT THE HORIZON.

By focusing your attention broadly, not only will you capture the major details, but variations and unexpected changes will become more apparent.

Be fresh.

Let your gaze penetrate some unusual recess, then return to something nearby. When you find a strange, new point in the scene, let your eyes linger there, then return to the entire setting. Explore visually but keep using your peripheral vision to absorb the whole.

We spend most of our waking hours staring, and we tend to stare at objects which we have looked at before. Looking at a familiar scene our eyes focus unconsciously but persistently on objects which we already know. The familiar crowds out the fresh!

Walk along a commonly used path.

Make a conscious effort to avoid looking at the familiar objects. Focus broadly. Look up more often. Visually capture the whole pathway.

FILLING

ACCENTUATE THE NEGATIVE.

Find a lone tree.

Sit down far enough away so you can take in the whole tree at a glance. Visually explore this tree. Examine its trunk and branches and foliage. Let your gaze move along a branch, down the trunk, up again into the leaves. Pause on some particular limb or feature. Take your time. Try to capture the exact shape of the tree.

Now let your gaze shift to the spaces around and BEHIND the tree. Instead of focusing on the tree itself, focus on the spaces BE-TWEEN its branches. Note how your tree suddenly seems to take on a new life, to fill out, to become whole. It practically leaps forward in taking on a new dimension.

A tree is not just its trunk, and branches, and leaves. It's a whole - - a multi-faceted, living, reaching, growing, organism. It is more than the sum of its parts. A tree IS its surroundings.

Look at your tree again.

Focus on the space between two branches -- the EXACT shape of no-branch.

SOLIDS ILLUMINATE SPACES. Branch and no-branch. Tree and no-tree. Solid and no-solid. Space and no-space. Each is known only in terms of the other. Or to put it another way, "you cannot have mountains without valleys."

SURVEYING

EXAMINE THINGS FROM VARYING VIEWPOINTS.

Select a stationary object to survey -- something you've "looked at" many times before.

Survey your object by peering at it from various angles. Move around. Get down on your hands and knees. Change your position. Lie down on your back. Turn your head to the side.

THE FAMILIAR IS THE UNFAMILIAR FROM A DIFFERENT VANTAGE POINT. One thing is many things. An object presents as many different faces as there are points to view it from.

Walk into scenes.

Get behind objects. Get under them -- above them.

We tend to view everything in one-dimensional terms. Life is not an art gallery!

Pick an object you can hold in your hand.

Hold it at varying distances from your eyes. Set it down and walk around it. Lie down and place it on your cheek. Let it rest on your chest, over your eye. Now set it down and look at it as part of its surroundings. How does it view its neighbors? How do its neighbors view it?

OBSERVING

LET THE NATURAL WORLD ENGULF YOU.

Locate a comfortable spot where you can lean back against something. Fold your hands loosely in your lap -- slightly cupped -- one inside the other. You may want to cross your ankles. Loosen any tight clothing.

Now take two or three deep breaths and as you exhale, let your body relax -- SETTLE IN.

Become completely motionless.

Don't strain, but try not to move at all. Just freeze. Let the natural world sweep over you.

Within fifteen minutes you should begin to feel as if you're being engulfed. The life of the community takes up where it left off. Squirrels may play around your feet, deer poke inquisitive heads into your clearing, birds alight on your shoes! This is seton-watching; a technique designed after the observation emphasis of the naturalist, Ernest Thompson Seton. It is not possible to describe the unitive feeling of wholeness which sweeps over the seton-watcher.

Go out and experience it for yourself.

ORCHESTRATING

USE ALL OF YOUR SENSES TO FUSE THE FACETS OF AWARENESS.

Find a private, quiet spot.

Add successive dimensions of awareness as you absorb this whole, marvelous personal space. Be polysensory. Revel in your surroundings.

Gulp the air.

Savor its taste and smell. Soak in its sounds. Flow with your feelings.

Loosen your body.

Stretch your arms up over your head. Rise up on tip-toes. Breathe deeply. Hunch your shoulders. Let your arms dangle. Shake loose the muscles of arms and legs.

Spread your toes.

Take off your shoes and socks. Now, grip the earth with your feet.

Tilt your head back.

Run your hand up the back of your neck -- fingers through your hair.

Scan the horizon.

Turn around. Reach out to pull in the colors. Take off some clothing.

Spread your fingers.

Turn your palms up to the elements. Raise your arms slightly. Absorb. Suck it all up like a dry sponge.

YOU ARE AN ORCHESTRA.

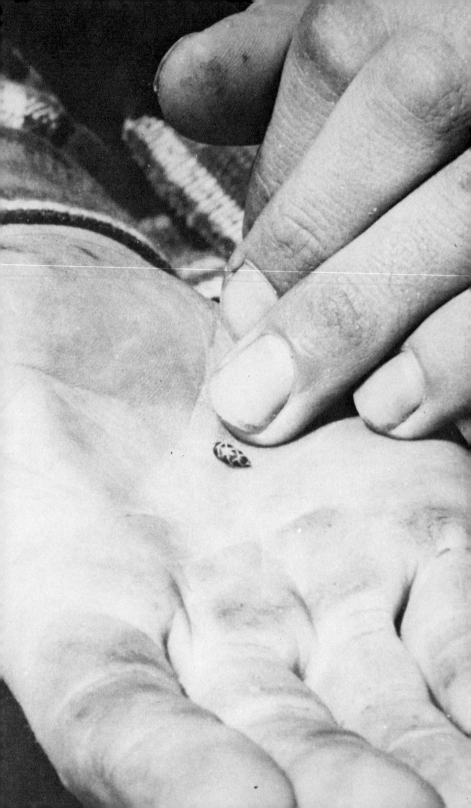

SCRUTINIZING

LOOK FOR THE SMALL THINGS.

Select an object which you can hold in your hand. Examine it minutely -- as if you were going to have to locate it in a pile of twenty other objects just like it. Really get to know it. Use all of your senses.

Think: what if I could not see it, could I still locate it in a pile of identical items? Would I know it by its smell or taste or sound?

Pick a natural setting. Sit down and begin scrutinizing your place with the same thoroughness as you did with your object. Explore it visually. Use all of your senses to absorb its special blend.

Places and things may be similar, but they are always different. Nothing is really LIKE anything else. Every thing and every place has its own fresh qualities -- that by which a thing is what it is. And such small things provide richness as well as variety in the fabric of life.

Discover the unique elements of your place.

Change your angle. Turn around and around. Crawl in widening circles. Picture in your mind how your place would look on a map. How would it appear to a leprechaun? In your mind's eye, can you see it as a giant would?

SMALL THINGS COUNT.

EMPATHIZING

ROLE-PLAY NATURAL QUALITIES.

Observe a tree.

Try to feel its "woodiness," or its "greenness," or its "tallness," just by looking at it. Get inside its substance.

We identify with something by sharing experiences. We feel "at home with" something by sharing surroundings.

Put your arms around your tree.

Hug it. Clasp it to your body. Smell its skin. Trace the patterns in its bark with your fingertips.

We role-play to gain contact with inner and outer feelings. How the object feels gives depth to how you feel.

Watch an animal.

Enter into its feelings in the same way. What does it see? How does the sun feel on its back? Become this animal's friend -- waiting on him to come and play. Tag along with him.

YOU ARE WHAT YOU FEEL. One way to get outside yourself is to get INSIDE something else. By giving your whole self to the experience it will fill your world.

SILENCING

WORK AT TURNING OFF THAT TINY VOICE IN THE BACK OF YOUR HEAD.

Sit down.
Just enjoy being alive.
Neither the past, nor the future can take the place of this moment. It's not "there and then," but "here and now."
Don't hold on.
It's not easy to shut off your mental broadcaster and just receive. It's not ignoring it, but just not dwelling upon it, that counts.
Don't try too hard.
Forget about making sense out of things.
Just let them happen. Let experience elect its own pace. TAKE THINGS AS THEY ARE. Awareness is being there.
Let it flow.
Choose some time like this each day when you just sit down and watch. Enjoy the freshness. Relax. Let meanings seep away. Quiet yourself.
These minutes are unique. They can never be repeated. Relish them.

WAITING

BECOME AN EMPTY VESSEL WAITING TO BE FILLED.

Let it come.

Relax. You can think about the future if you want -- or reminisce in the past -- just don't let either dominate your day. DON'T PUSH.

You cannot hurry the coming of tomorrow.

Let it be.

Take each day in its turn -- breathe each hour to the fullest. Don't talk, do.

Energy flows from the sun. It bathes the surface of this whirling mass. It gives life. You are part of that flow -- a piece of the sun -- a tiny, warm, speck of life.

Bask in the natural elements and the natural rhythms.

The nature of life is nature. Each day is a growing day.

A QUIET WALK

It's like taking off into a dream.
The water starts at the trees and stretches way out there. The clouds are forming the islands.
It goes way out instead of up!
The way the clouds are jagged is like the way trees are jagged-- they really look like mountains with trees growing on them!

The sun has just gone down. It's that quiet time of day, when the wind is beginning to die away and the waves in the lake smooth themselves into calm, unhurried ripples. The setting sun draws behind it a sheet of faint, salmon light that hovers over the horizon. Above, the sky is still dimly blue. The tips of the pines glow in the reflected light, but beneath, in the growing shadows, they blend into darkness. A few clouds hang motionless above the trees.

We are standing on a boardwalk that reaches out into the marsh, and we're watching that sky. The boys are describing the "seascapes in the air" that Jim brought them out here to see.

An hour later, we sit in a circle among a grove of pines to share our experiences. The lighting has faded. The seascapes have been blotted out. The forest has changed. . .

I was sitting there facing the lake and an otter came swimming right toward me! I heard him splashing before I saw him, and then saw him moving through the water. Then he splashed again and disappeared.

I heard bats coming out. One flew right over me! They were flying all around above my head.

There was something crawling on the ground near me. I heard it, but I didn't know what it was. It squirmed right under my foot!

I was sitting and just listening. Then I heard this laugh--kind of a screeching. I think it was maybe a loon, but it was weird.

The mist was coming up on the lake. I watched it moving in.

I saw the night world coming in. The bats and the mosquitoes start coming in as it gets dark. It changes--all the birds were leaving.

Look at the moon. I was watching it.

The night world is really half--I don't usually think about it as being half, but it's really just as much as the day.

Finally, in this very place, but several hours earlier, we had seen another world, an entirely different one. . . .

In the early morning the wind is blowing, and I feel like running with the wind. I have a good feeling in the morning. It goes away as I get tired. At night, I start getting rested, and in the morning I get the good feeling again.

I feel free in the morning. During the day I start feeling "jailed up" inside. But in the morning I feel free.

The birds were all singing. Like they were saying, "Good Morning!"

The air feels crisp and clean against our cheeks. We're standing on the boardwalk, trying to absorb that special freshness of a day that's just beginning. The sky is clear, blue, and far, far away. The wind is yawning through the trees as we, too, yawn and stretch, "waking up" to morning. We reach out and try to pull it in. Stretching IN. Breathing silence. Opening ourselves up to newness. Now, the sun is beginning to peek through the trees, as though it has just rolled out of a warm cloud-bed itself.

For the next hour we walk, turn into movie cameras, become bees and butterflies, squint, role-play animals. Look for homes, describe things from different angles, hatch like a baby bird, burst out of a cover of leaves like a mushroom, and wash our hands in the soil. We sit silently for a while, alone with the trees and sky and sun and the life all around. Then we get back together to share our feelings and what we have experienced. We explore and discover and share the world together.

There are many techniques that can be used in a Quiet Walk sequence. Some are specifically suited to the world of dawn, others to the world of night; but most can be used any time.

MOVIE CAMERA. Concentrate on SEEING by becoming movie cameras. One of the most delicate and amazing lenses in the world is the lens in the human eye. So become cameras:

Wide-angle lens - looking straight ahead, hold your arms out to your sides at eye-level. While still looking straight ahead, slowly bring your arms forward. Stop movement when you can first see both thumbs. That's your widest range of vision. Now drop your arms. Using this wide lens, "pan" by letting your eyes play on the horizon, not stopping to focus on anything. Just constantly move them along the line of trees and sky.

Telephoto lens - use cardboard sighting tubes to zero in and concentrate on a small fragment of the scene.

Macro lens - hold your closed fist up against one eye like a jeweler's monocle and look through it at small objects held close.

Colored lenses - look at the world through lenses made of various colors of cellophane. How different and new everything is with a filter of color!

Squint - put the camera out of focus to see lines and patterns without the confusion of details; then slowly bring your eyes back into focus until they click into a clear picture. In the forest, let your eyes be swept upwards to the canopy.

Upside down - bend and look at things upside down, between your legs, toddler-style.

These "movie camera" techniques may be used at intervals along the trail, suiting the lens to the scene to be focused upon. Be sure you "turn off" the camera before emphasizing other senses.

HANDWASHING. Stop at various places and wash your hands in the soil, leaves, sand, marsh water, moss, rotting wood--anything and everything. Wash fronts, backs, sides, palms, fingers, wrists. Feel with the entire hand. This is a good way to compare different kinds of "the stuff that's on the ground!"

PRICKLY - TICKLY. Divide up into groups of three. Have each person find something with prickles and find something that tickles. (Everyone should keep his discoveries secret until it is time for "sending.") The "receiving" member sits with his hands in his lap, palms up and head tilted back, eyes closed. The other two silently and slowly share their objects by patting them lightly in his palm, brushing them along his cheek, and rubbing them under his chin several times. Switch roles so everyone gets to be a receiver.

SYMPHONY. Have the group lie down like spokes of a wheel, feet in the center. Ask them to close their eyes and just listen for a couple of minutes to the various sounds. Then say that usually, when we listen, we attach names to things and think: that's a bird; that's the wind; that's the water on the shore; that's a chipmunk scuttling along the forest floor. Try not to identify the sounds now, but just let them flow into your mind and blend together, like all the different instruments in a symphony. Instead of naming the sounds, describe them with letters. ("wind" becomes whhirrrrr. . .) Let the sounds move you and maybe even seemingly lift you up to float quietly for a few moments. Do this for a couple of minutes. Then concentrate on the sounds drifting in and fading out--the crescendos and decrescendos of a symphony orchestra. Now, try to MAKE the sounds come in and go out by tuning in on one instrument, then another.

NEGATIVE SPACES. Sit down facing a tree, just far enough away so you can see the whole tree in one "eyeful" without having to move your head. First, let your eyes explore the trunk; then move out along the branches and leaves. Let your eyes follow the way the tree is growing. Take your time. Now, shift your focus and look at the spaces around the tree--where the tree ISN'T. Focus on the holes between the branches and between the leaves. Note how the tree seems to leap forward. It becomes three-dimensional, and the space around it as well as the space it takes up seem to merge into one living whole.

WAKING-UP. This is especially good in the morning. Stand in the sunlight, lined up arm's lengths apart. Usually, when we wake up, we stretch out, reaching our arms high and wide. So go ahead and stretch out. Rise up on tip-toes to reach for the sky. Now, take three big deep breaths of this morning air, and stretch IN, trying to pull into yourself this whole feeling of morning. Get it. Absorb it. Wake up to it. Take it back with you, to have for the rest of the day!

SHARING CIRCLE. At the end of a Quiet Walk form a sharing circle. Stand in a circle, holding hands; sit down, go around the circle having each person verbalize his feelings, observations, or sensory experiences. It gives everybody a chance to tell about the "neatest thing that happened," and it makes a nice summary of the Quiet Walk.

ANGLES. Place each member of the group in a different position or at a different angle to some object, perhaps an old stump, a tree, or a large rock. Ask each person to describe to the group what the object looks like from his vantage point. How does it look from different sides? From ground level? From a higher perspective? From far away? From very close up. (Or looking between his legs, sitting on someone's shoulders, lying on his back?) Ask everyone to rotate, every few minutes, changing his angle, or ask each person to describe for the group what he sees using just two or three words. (Copy the words down for a poem.)

HATCHING. Sit in a circle; turn around, so that you face outward (rather than inward looking at each other). Curl up as if you are inside an eggshell. Feel the shell closing you in. The shell is the old "you." It's your barrier to awareness. Now begin to hatch. Strain against the sides of the shell to break free. Peck at the shell with your nose. Make a crack; start a small opening. Struggle to get out; break the shell. Emerge! Alive--free--open--reborn! Glorious.

COLOR CHAINS. Have everyone collect small pieces of leaves, but take them all from one primary color category, like only pieces of RED leaves. Take along an old belt or a strip of cardboard and some glue. Attach the pieces -- overlapping to form a color chain -- beginning with the lightest red and ending with the darkest. This is a good technique in late summer or fall when you find a variety of colors in similar leaves.

SEASCAPES. Evening is really the time to observe seascapes. Get a clear view of the sky, with clouds above the horizon. Now shift your mental idea of the horizon until it is ABOVE the clouds, and see the clouds and lower part of the sky as extending out to this more distant horizon. The sky becomes an ocean. The clouds are islands, with trees and inlets and mountains. Often you can even see the "horizon" beyond them if there is a line in the sky where the lighting and color is different, like a change from pink to blue. Let your eyes sail on that ocean, in and out among the islands and harbors. Take a fantasy journey to distant lands as you sail across the "sea in the sky."

ANT'S-EYE VIEW. This is done with one person at a time. Lie down, face up, in tall grass or clumps of moss--anywhere that the ground vegetation can surround your head. Shut your eyes and feel along the ground with your fingers, like an ant walking across the forest floor; walk with your hands. Stretch out your arms. Pretend they are the antennae of the ant (keep fingers and thumb together). Explore and probe around your habitat with your new "eyes." Now open

63

your eyes and look up at the people standing around you looking down on YOU. Turn your head to the side and peer out through the vegetation right at ground level; shut your topmost eye and just look with the ground level one. Now find a real ant and follow him for a while.

SETON STOOLS. These are special "sitting places"--natural spots located next to an old log, or tree trunk, or boulder--where a person can lean back and just quietly take it all in. Use them for SETON-WATCHING (sitting absolutely still for at least twenty minutes to let everything settle down around you), or for pretending that you are a tiny amphibian, peering at the world from atop your *toadstool.*

LISTENING POSTS. Ask each person to find a special "listening" tree nearby. By putting their ear up to the tree they can focus on all the sounds of the forest. After a couple minutes of listening, have them share the sounds they picked up. Then ask everyone to sit down next to their listening post and write down what they hear, but only as *letters* describing each of the sounds. No names, just letters strung together. On a sheet of paper have them show their listening post with these sound waves coming in from different directions.

IMAGES. Sit in a circle and pass around some natural object. As each person receives the leaf, shell, pine cone, or whatever to examine; he must describe it. But each in turn must describe it differently from the way anyone else did. Some might look at it from different angles; some might talk about its color, or its shape, its smell, its taste, its texture, or its sound. Some might even describe its feelings or its place. (You may want to call out "pass" every couple of minutes to regulate the pace.) When all have finished with the object say: "Let's return it very carefully to its natural spot. If you ever walk by here again, you'll probably recognize it and feel as if you know it."

AMBULATORS. These are exercises to do while walking:

Passing it back - pick up something that is interesting and pass it to the person behind you. He passes it on, and so forth to the end.

Walking backwards - especially effective where there is a natural "hallway" such as a deer run. Just turn around and walk for a while facing where you've been instead of where you're going. It slows down the pace and changes the vantage point.

Going barefoot - don't overlook the obvious sensory advantages of taking off your shoes and socks. You can pause along the way and try to pick up different objects with your toes.

Looking for a color - when there's going to be a fairly long walk between techniques, ask everyone to watch for a specific color (pick a color, any color!) and to point out things that are that color. This can also be done with PATTERNS, or ASSOCIATIONS (spirals, something helping something else, etc.).

Movie camera - the wide angle lens of the movie camera technique can also be used as you are moving along a trail.

Animal tracks - say, "From here to there (specify there), we'll all walk like different animals." Each person chooses what animal he wants to be--an animal that might live in the area. Then, each person walks like his animal, thinking about the kind of tracks that animal would make.

CRAYONS. Take pre-outlined sheets of paper and clipboards along for coloring. Have the participants "color" their scenes with plant juices and pollen, or tiny bits of leaves and bark stuck on with tree sap. Or, take a single sheet of paper along and have everyone contribute to a group composition. The idea is to focus on color not collage. Save the latter for another day.

WHEELS. For quiet, close-in sharing, have the group lie down like the spokes of a wagon wheel. It is important for everyone in the circle to be touching. Have them on their backs for personal revelations, on their stomachs for focusing on something small. Sharing in this fashion can include focusing on sounds, overhead leaves and clouds, colors and patterns, etc., or on questions of environmental values, flights of imagination and spirit. Compare the structural arrangement of your "wheel" to the whole world.

PERCHES. Ask each member of the group "What is your favorite animal in this area?" or "What animal would you most like to be like?" Then take the person to a "perch" appropriate for that animal and ask him to role-play alone the animal he has chosen; try to absorb the surroundings as the animal might. Follow this personal task with a group sharing opportunity or ask each person to act out his experience for the others.

FRIENDS. Pick up a leaf, a rock, a stick, a pine cone--anything that you see that you like and can pick up with one hand. Something that strikes you as being neat--that you would like to make friends with--just pick it up and let it tag along with you. Smell it. Taste it. Rub it on your cheek. Hold it up to the light and look at it from different angles. Lie down and put it on your forehead to feel its weight. Put it on your eyelid, your mouth, your chest. Close your eyes and just feel it. Really get to know it. Rub it on your ear; listen to it. You might want to make friends with more than one object. You might want one to keep, one to hide somewhere so you can come back and find it, and one to give to someone else.

ECHOING. Improvise a dance to celebrate the life of a plant or an animal. Imitate the motions of a fawn gamboling along a beach, or a plant slowly turning its leaves toward the sunlight, or a bird feeding its young. It doesn't have to be an exact representation. In your own human way, you can symbolize these activities in a kind of dance; and just as an echo replies with a variation of the original voice, your echoing can be your reply, your salute, to the moment of life you want to commemorate.

BEES AND BUTTERFLIES. Become bees or butterflies and explore a flowery area as they would. Zig-zag from one blossom to another. Use your nose. Watch the bees and butterflies for clues. Feel the texture of petals on your face; taste the pollen. Feel free of the earth; seem to fly as you dart from one spot to another. Afterwards gather around the honey pot for a "bit of honey" and share your feelings. Were you a person thinking about being a butterfly, or a butterfly thinking about being a person?

HELPERS. Divide the group into teams of two. One partner spends five minutes repeating the phrase "I am aware . . ." and filling in the sentence. The other person helps him stay in the present by stopping him if he slips out of the "here and now," and keeping him focused on what's happening right at that moment. After a couple of minutes, the helper should encourage the player to be aware of *his own feelings,* too. (Not what he *thinks,* but how does he *feel.*) Then have the partners switch roles and repeat.

ONE-OF-A-KIND. Each person is given a particular kind of leaf. Tell them to examine it so carefully that they would be able to pick it out of a whole pile of such leaves. During the next five minutes, they look at it, feel it, hold it at different angles, etc. Then put all the leaves together--with some identical leaves that no one has explored--and have them find theirs. It's one of a kind! Afterwards, ask them to explain to the group what makes their leaf unique. Then ask them to share what makes them unique. (You may want to suggest that they take their "one of a kind" leaf and mail it in a special letter to a "one of a kind" friend.)

NATURAL OBSERVATION SPOTS. These are places where you can station persons to observe the action. Find spots near special animal homes--a bird's nest, an ant hill, near a muskrat lodge or bee's hive, or close to the home of a squirrel or chipmunk. Just watch. See what the animal does. Follow it. (Instruct everyone to leave an offering behind near their animal's home--like a special stick, a crumb of food, or a plaything!)

SILENT PARTNERS. This technique can be used after any individual activity. It is good for breaking through the "words for things" barrier. Divide the group into pairs. Ask the partners to share their experience using nonverbal communication. Afterwards, ask them to go off by themselves and just sit quietly together for a while-- *with shoulders touching*--watching the natural world.

VIEWING PARTIES. Borrowing on an old idea from the Japanese, plan a party just to sit and watch the moon rise. Look in an almanac to find the date when a new moon will be rising. Station yourselves somewhere with a good, open view. Then sit silently and watch the moon rise as a huge orange disc. Wait until it has risen and faded into a normal-sized white moon. During this time, write poems (haiku) and then share them with the group.

Stay up late--or get up at, say, 1:00 a.m. to watch the stars on a clear night. Lie down in an open field and just look up. See the stars first as a canopy--then focus on a bright star in the middle of the Milky Way and begin to see the earth in perspective--you're on a planet that is located on a flat plane of which that star is the center. Or look for patterns in the stars, as ancient people did.

Check an almanac for predicted meteor showers. Take sleeping bags out to an open area where you can lie and look up. Concentrate on one sector of the sky--you'll see the "shooting stars" as they pass through.

Or just take time to really watch a sunset. Take writing or sketching materials if you wish, and give a poem or a drawing to a friend, but the main thing at a viewing party is quiet watchfulness--a certain reverance for an act of life. It is not necessary to DO anything at a viewing party. It is just warmth and companionship in the midst of existence.

Have a sun watch. This is an all-night vigil, resembling the ceremonies of some American Indian tribes. Keep a campfire going all night--perhaps several campfires, all along a lakeshore. Then, when the first rays of light appear, send runners through camp to awaken everyone. In silence, all gather to watch the coming of the sun.

BUDDING. This is an exercise that is particularly good in the early morning. Sit in a circle. Then turn the circle around so everyone is facing OUT, rather than in. Now, become like the bud of a flower or a tree. Start by pulling in knees and arms and hunching over, all curled up into a tight ball. Slowly, slowly open to the sunshine. Gradually unfold. Shake your head and loosen your shoulders. Reach out.

Or be buried in a pile of leaves to become a mushroom. First one finger on each hand pokes up through the layer, then one more finger at a time until the whole hand pops up. Then the arms spring up; a head pokes through. Finally, like a mushroom on a warm day after the rain, come bursting out from the earth! Explode!

TREETOPS. Sit down at a spot where everyone can see the tops of the trees in the distance. It will help if they can see along a plane extending among the treetops (not looking *up* but *in*). Let the crowns of the trees pull you in visually. The tops of trees are where their personalities take flight. What is happening there? Picture yourself as sitting on one of those upper branches. What do you see? (Or, imagine that you are one of those birds flying among the foliage.)

GALLERY. This is usually an activity for the end of a sequence. It is a good way to bring a Quiet Walk to a close. First, pass out clipboards, paper, and pencils or pens. Then, walk out to the natural observation spots. Instruct each person situated at a spot to absorb his surroundings and to express what he feels and what he senses while he is there. Explain that there are many means of expression using pencil and paper. One can write words, use symbols, sketch, or try poetry or haiku. After 15-30 minutes, have the group join up again and have a gallery. This isn't like most art galleries, all closed in with painted walls. It's nature's gallery, with trees for walls and the sky for a ceiling--and perhaps a plush moss carpet or a floor of pine needles. Hang the gallery pieces--whatever was done for self-expression--on trees, by wedging them under a piece of bark or sticking a twig through them or poking a bunch of pine needles through. Then have a tour of the gallery, with each artist explaining his own work and interpreting and sharing his feelings to the others. Remember, there is no such thing as "constructive" criticism. Everyone's self-expression is GOOD.

SHARING WALK. Split the group into teams of two. One member wears a blindfold, the other guides him into sensory experiences. The guide has a double task: to seek out interesting touch, sound, smell, and taste sensations in the surroundings; AND to help the other person appreciate them with no verbal communication. The guide can lead, pull, manipulate fingers, roll the person on the ground, hold objects up to his friend's nose or mouth, gently move objects to and fro, cup a hand over the other's ear and snap a twig right next to it, and so on. After five to ten minutes, switch places so that each member of the pair has a chance both to lead and to follow.

ALIASES. Forming a circle at the end of a Quiet Walk, ask "what animal that lives in this area would you most like to be able to turn into?" Go around the circle and let each disclose his preferred "alias." Then ask each person why he chose that animal--what qualities does the animal have that he admires the most?

Or, ask everyone to close their eyes and pretend that they are a tree. They should think about where they are growing, how their branches look, what is the color and shape of their bark, foliage, and roots, etc. After a few minutes, ask each person to describe his "treeness" to the group.

WHISPERS. Join hands to form a circle and sit down. Begin by tilting your head to the side and saying, "Listen very carefully. Can you hear the plants whispering?" After pausing for a few moments, ask "If they had words, what would their words be?" Go around the circle, asking them to give examples. "What is the moss saying to the fern?" or "What does the pine tree share with the maple tree?" or "How do the wildflowers feel about the wind?"

MAKING FRIENDS WITH A BUTTERFLY. This takes patience, but it's worth it. Moisten a little sugar with saliva and hold it on your finger. Try to get a butterfly to alight there. Find a butterfly that is on a flower, and slowly, gently, place the sugar-watered finger next to it. If you move slowly, and wait, and maneuver a little, you can make friends with a butterfly.

GETTING TO KNOW A TREE. Put on blindfolds to heighten other senses. After a short spin (just like in pin-the-tail-on-the-donkey) to erase the sense of direction, guide each participant to a tree. Any tree. Ask him to explore it. Hug it. Rub his cheek against it. Listen to it--try to hear the life inside it, the sap running, the life breathing within. Explore its "skin" with tongue, fingers, nose, his own skin. Check out its base--where it grows. Is anything living on it? After each gets to know his tree, lead them away again. Then, take the blindfolds off, return to the general area, and let each camper try to find "his" tree. They probably will. Some make a beeline for it right away, some scratch their heads and run a gamut of tests--size, shape, texture, moss on the trunk--but they always end by patting the trunk and affirming: "THIS is MINE!"

The Quiet Walk provides a format for those who are interested in a slow-paced, discovery-oriented medium. It combines the best aspects of the field trip--spontaneity, openness, and lack of time structuring--with sensory ingredients, mechanical insights, and specific inputs. The Quiet Walk is free-flowing, yet retains a commitment to gaining total participation through specialized techniques. The slower pace lends itself to opportunities for empathizing ("budding like a flower"), sharing ("describing your experience non-verbally"), and expressing ("creating a dance to celebrate the life of a plant") as well as sensing and discovering.

The variety of techniques allows for many different Quiet Walks along the same trail, and a person could go on several Quiet Walks and have unique experiences on each occasion. Times of day are important, in that the Quiet Walk was designed to take advantage of special moments--early morning and dusk, with occasional forays into the later evening hours. Most of the techniques are obviously appropriate for any hour. The morning and evening simply add a bit of magic to the atmosphere.

Unlike the field trip or the interpretive walk, the format of the Quiet Walk is designed to gain full participation. One of our original ACC discoveries was that typically the participants on a field trip would array themselves in concentric circles of interest-involvement around the leader. The members of the innermost ring would be touching one another or the leader himself; those in the next ring -- at three foot away -- would be facing the inner cluster but not necessarily looking in that direction; at a twelve foot radius one or two members would neither be facing nor looking towards the action; and usually at the twenty foot mark one lone member stood hunched over, hands in pockets, precariously balanced on a dry hummock of turf! We knew, intuitively, that what we really wanted to achieve was the close-in involvement of those members in the central cluster. So we began experimenting with ways of pulling everyone into the innermost ring. Our motivators ran the gamut: stimulating, cajoling, enticing, manipulating, including. And, in time, our product achieved a unique sense of wholeness. A good Quiet Walk is like a good wine: it's exhilarating in its approach, revealing in its play, and warm in its afterglow.

The Quiet Walk can serve as a sensory introduction to the environment for those who do not have the opportunity to participate in the six-day Acclimatization experience. In this function, it far surpasses the ordinary limits of a field trip or interpretive walk. The Quiet

Walk is also an excellent supplement to an existing ACC program for those who want to do more. Sensory interaction with the environment is a process, not a final product. The Quiet Walk continues that process.

quiet walk   **the guidelines**

general

- plan the format for the Quiet Walk ahead of time. Walk the trail that will be used, noting good locations for specific activities such as the GALLERY, SEASCAPES, SETON STOOLS, and NEGATIVE SPACES. Select the techniques to form a sequence mixing those from different groupings and filling in between with AMBULATORS. (Plan on moving to a different spot for each exercise.) Include one of the techniques from the "sharing" group for the close. Keep the whole thing down to an hour or an hour and a half.

- the Quiet Walk should not be a hike; nor should it be absolutely silent -- quiet can also mean "low-key."

- many of the techniques begin with a circle. To form a circle, have the group hold hands. It's really the only quick way to insure getting both a circle and total participation.

groupings

Sensing	Empathizing	Sharing
movie camera	hatching	sharing circle
handwashing	ant's-eye view	wheels
prickly-tickly	perches	silent partners
symphony	echoing	gallery
negative spaces	bees and butterflies	sharing walk
waking-up	viewing parties	aliases
angles	budding	whispers
color chains		
seascapes		
seton stools		
listening posts		
images		
ambulators		
crayons		
friends		
helpers		
one-of-a-kind		
natural observation spots		
treetops		
making friends with a butterfly		
getting to know a tree		

preparation
- sign the group up beforehand and give them a general briefing on what will happen. For a morning walk, mention:

    "lay out your clothes the night before, fireman style. When you are awakened in the morning, jump quickly and quietly into your clothes, wash your face and hands, and meet at . . . (a designated central location). To avoid waking others and to convey the tone of quietude, have only non-verbal communication until you arrive at the meeting place."

- make arrangements to have the group awakened, or wake them up yourself.
- when the campers arrive at the meeting spot, talk quietly, using your best hushed voice.
- have a toast to the morning with a glass of cold, fresh juice, before starting.
- if insects are a potential disruptive element, provide a good insect repellent and take charge of its application. This is especially important if seton-watching, perches, or natural observation techniques will be used.
- SETON STOOLS, NATURAL OBSERVATION SPOTS, and PERCHES depend upon good locations. You may want to build actual seats. These should either have backs or be propped up against a natural backrest (tree or rock). You can also place some up in the trees--with hanging rope ladders!

sensing
- for MOVIE CAMERAS you may want to hold up one hand, closed into a cylinder, and use this as your "lens" while you crank away with your other hand. Make sighting tubes from empty paper towel or toilet paper tubes--these become "telephoto" lenses. When "squinting," talk through it: "Do you see the vertical lines? Let your eyes follow the basic lines of the scene."
- during WAKING-UP and SEASCAPES, campers may spontaneously relate what they feel; encourage this, because what they relate can help others, who will build upon these expressions.
- for ANGLES, have the campers position themselves at different distances from the object. Some may come up with unusual perspectives, like standing on their heads or on someone's shoulders. Then have them switch places with one another. Suggest that they might want to stop by and look at their object at night.
- for FRIENDS, SYMPHONY, and NEGATIVE SPACES watch the pace. Go slowly enough to give them time to absorb.
- for IMAGES, keep the descriptions short--one to two minute limit--just a few words per participant; this gives the last guy a little better chance!
- in FRIENDS, ask "How do you make friends with people?" "How does a casual acquaintance become an intimate friend?"

empathizing
- you'll probably only want to use one of these per Quiet Walk; they take 5 - 15 minutes each.
- use these as the next-to-last technique in the sequence, followed by a SHARING CIRCLE.

- for ECHOING, encourage use of the entire body--there are some good guidelines for modern dance that might help.
- in BEES AND BUTTERFLIES, have girls become bees and boys become butterflies--a little role-reversal makes the exercise even more interesting! Also, have an open area, preferably a meadow or field, where participants can be somewhat alone, decreasing the element of self-consciousness. Join hands and sit in a circle at the beginning of the exercise while it is explained. Begin by suggesting that everyone imagine in their mind's-eye the flight of a honeybee or a butterfly. Then the leader goes around the circle symbolically placing a "magic mask" (invisible) over each participant's face and explaining in the process that this device will aid in losing self-consciousness, and decreasing ego vibrations.
- timing is important for empathizing exercises. It is usually best to explain the procedure, and let everyone do it at their own pace. If this doesn't feel comfortable, talk them through the exercise. The latter has one advantage, in that everyone gets through at about the same time. However, let them know if you'll be talking them through it--or just explaining it for them ahead of time, to do on their own. This avoids having someone sitting immobile, waiting for you to tell him what to do!

- for PERCHES, it's good to have different kinds of locations: an amphibian might be near the lake, a reptile in the grass, a bird perched on a stump or windfall.

sharing

- have blindfolds ready and on hand for the SHARING WALK. We use costume masks, purchased at a novelty shop; the eyeholes are covered by two thicknesses of opaque tape. These, because of the elastic head-straps, are easier to use than cloth blindfolds, and generally are harder to peek through.

- when using the GALLERY technique, you will find it easiest to walk out along the trail dropping each person off at his spot, then take the final spot for yourself. Afterwards, you can retrace your route picking up each of the others as you return.

- distribute clipboards, paper, and felt-tipped pens for the natural observation part of the GALLERY, but keep the sharing portion as a surprise. Creative expression tends to be more spontaneous and less self-conscious when it is not intended for other eyes. Then, if someone really doesn't want to put his paper in the gallery, he doesn't have to-- but when every one is sharing, most people join in and honestly share. The GALLERY is no time to play art critic or poetry critic, neither for the leader nor for the participants. It's sharing. Be reinforcing.

- when people share, they tend to talk to the leader and ignore others. The SHARING CIRCLE helps somewhat, but you may need to encourage them to direct their sharing and relating to the whole group. Go from person to person in turn, and positively reinforce any statement made. If your group has difficulty in really expressing their deeper feelings, try WHEELS (on your backs).

AN ENVIRONMENTAL STUDY STATION

Cool!
There's stuff growing here.
It smells . . . old.
It doesn't taste so great, either.
It's big, I'll say that much.
Mossy -- this must be moss.
It's soft.
But it's hard, too.
It's really weird.
It's really neat!

They're grokking the rock.

Five boys are standing, barefooted and blindfolded, right in front of a huge boulder. Standing isn't really the word, though, for although their feet are stationary, their bodies are moving. With the palms of their hands they press, pat, and stroke the obstacle in front of them; they sniff it and rub their cheeks and noses and ears against it. Some of the more adventuresome even snake out their tongues to use their sense of taste. Their minds are busy, along with their senses, trying to explore and understand what this object is.

Following the sound of Jim's voice, they walk all around it, return to their original spots, and then are led away from the rock again. We talk about what "the thing" might be:

At first I thought it was a tree, but then I could feel that it was made of stone. Then I found this one chunk, and it was heavy, so then I knew it was rock.

Grokking is one of the experiences at the Environmental Study Station, a primitive campsite surrounded by marsh on three sides, with the lake on the other. Ten boys -- a cabin group -- go with the two trippers to this site for a three-day "campout" that is different from all other campouts. Besides learning how to live in the out-of-doors, they study the environment in unique, and fun, ways. They grok, build micro-trails, ramble, collect, investigate seeds, emerge from cocoons, and think about environmental values. The Environmental Study Station takes advantage of living in the out-of-doors as an opportunity to learn about the natural world. There are several concepts at the core of the program:

energy flow -- all energy flows from the sun
land formation -- glaciers molded and shaped this land
soil formation -- soil is made from rocks and plants
homes -- everything has a home
adaptation -- everything grows to fit where and how it lives
communities -- plants and animals that need one another live
together
web of life -- all living things are connected

This is not pencil-and-paper environmental study -- just as it is not run-of-the-mill campcraft. The concepts are incorporated into the activities; in fact, everything that happens for three days can be tied into the concepts. The Environmental Study Station is a place for involvement with the environment.

THE MODEL. We're sitting in a circle in a sandy area of the campsite with our eyes closed. Jim reaches behind him into a duffle bag -- the "magic bag" -- to pull out an assortment of wooden blocks. When the campers open their eyes, they see a model of a campsite in the center of the circle. The "blocks" are now tents, a kitchen area, a fire ring, a woodpile, canoes, and a latrine.

"This is the Environmental Study Station. Now that we've arrived, we have to decide how we're going to live while we're out here. That's why we're having this community meeting. We really are a community here, because we each have different jobs, and we depend on each other for cooking and cleaning and building the fire and getting wood. We have to work together to take care of the things we all need. What would you say are some of the things we need while we're out here?"

Tents. "These green blocks represent our shelters, our tents. We'll put them up just about where they are in the model; we'll call that the shelter area. I think the community should decide who goes, in what tent, though, and who's going to put them up." After deciding on living arrangements, someone suggests, *Have everybody put up his own tent. Yeah. Build your own home.*

"Okay, what's another one of our needs?" *Food!* "All right, this is the kitchen area -- and the fire ring is part of the kitchen, too because that's where the food is cooked. This kitchen has a dirt floor, and it's easy to get dirt into the food while its being cooked. So I'd like to suggest a community ordinance -- that only the people on the cook crew be in the kitchen during cooking, so that dirt doesn't get kicked into the food." After a quick, and unanimous vote, one of the tent groups is assigned to the first shift at cooking.

"What's something besides food we need for cooking, though?"

Fire. Wood. "Okay, and this is the firewood pile. We'll have to collect lots of wood; one group will be on firewood and sanitation. We don't want to waste wood by burning more than we need, so these guys will be in charge of building the fire and putting wood in. Just the people who are fire-tenders add wood to the fire. And we have a saying 'If it goes in, it stays in.' That means, we don't play with firesticks because fire helps us live, but it can be destructive, too. And the firewood people are also in charge of digging the latrine. In our model, that will be over here."

After these mechanics have been gone over, and each group has a crew assignment, we introduce two additional slogans for the community. One is "Back up and re-group!" "When it's time for a community meeting, or when we're all scattered out and need to get together again, I'll call for a 'back up and regroup.' That means we'll all come back here and sit in the circle again. And another slogan -- if something goes wrong, instead of blaming somebody, let's just 'Deal with the situation.' It does a lot more good to try to take care of things than to hassle about whose fault it was."

The social community goes into action. And with the guidelines for outdoor living that we use, things run smoothly. The interdependencies transfer, too. By seeing themselves as a community, they begin to see more clearly how, for example, the forest community works.

THE SUN. "Back up and re-group!"

We form a circle at the community center. The tents are set up, the firewood is stacked, the latrine is dug, and all the gear has been moved in.

"There's one more thing we have to do to get camp set up. We've already taken care of most of our needs, but there's one more thing we need in order to live here. We have food and water and shelter and firewood -- but there's something we don't think about much that we need in order to live. We're going to put it up now. Let's move the circle over here."

Jim opens the "magic bag" again, this time removing a large, circular, tie-dyed cloth. "This is the sun. We're going to put it up to remind us of how important it is."

Each boy holds on to an edge of the sun while it is unfolded; they help carry it over to a large rope frame and place it carefully on the ground. Using small ropes, "rays", they all "hook up to the sun," tying it to the rope frame.

"Imagine that you're on a spaceship. There are certain things you'd have to have along in order to survive in outer space. You'd have to have everything on board that you need in order to live. You'd take a supply of food and water; big tanks of air; and you'd need a large supply of energy. If it was a long trip, you'd have to have ways of re-using some of the things you need -- re-cycling the materials you need to live -- and you'd have to have an almost unlimited supply of energy. You'd have to have *everything*. How many of you think you'll ever ride on a spaceship?"

Not me. I get airsick.

I want to!

Probably some day.

"Well, RIGHT NOW, we're all traveling through space in a

spaceship. We're carrying water and plants and animals and air and rocks and soil. We're on a planet that is like a spaceship, because everything that is needed for life has to be carried along. The atmosphere is like the walls of the spaceship, because nothing can live outside it. And we have limited supplies of some of our needs, too. There's a lot of air, but there's only so much and no more, and there's no way of getting more if we make this unfit to breathe. Same way with water -- there's a lot on board, but if we pollute it and make it unusable, there's no more water. Rocks, minerals, all the things we need, but only so much. So we have to re-cycle some of these things, too. Nature has a whole re-cycling system set up: it rains, the water runs into lakes, the lakes lose water to the air when it evaporates, the water in the air becomes clouds and falls again as rain. It's pretty neat when you think about it."

"The sun is the source of energy for our good ship, Earth. Without the sun, Tommy, you couldn't even rest your chin on your hand. And John, you couldn't smile without the sun's energy. None of us could be here if it weren't for that source of energy. It's the one thing we need that comes from outside the spaceship. So that's why, here, we want to 'put up the sun' to remind us of where all this power comes from, and also of how the earth is like a spaceship."

The sun is hoisted up between two trees like the sail of some strange vessel, the craft of an ancient sun-worshipping people. It will be a "hanging" focal point (literally) for the Environmental Study Station, forming the backdrop for everything else that happens. It's another sign that this is a special kind of camping trip -- and it is a reminder that the sun is always there and we depend on it.

"When somebody finds something cool, he can attach it to the sun, and when we do something special, we can put up one of these colored strands across the sun, like this, to remind us again that everything that lives on earth needs the sun."

MAGIC SPOTS. One of the main tasks of our first morning is for each camper to locate his own "magic" spot. Jim suggests that everyone will want to have a very special place where he can be by himself; a private place where each can go to be alone; a beautiful place that each can use in order to think or write or just sit and soak up his surroundings. It will be a quiet place for dreams, a secret place where each can explore his own feelings. Since this is a highly personal task, we don't talk about it much, but just go off quietly alone, alert to the discovery of our very own special magic spot.

My spot was really neat. It was towered over by a big pine and had walls of little spruce trees. The pine became my center of activity. I went over and talked to it. Of all that has happened, the pine had something to do with it. My tree was a very good friend. It kept the wind from blowing on me and making me cold. And it kept the sun from blinding me or making me too warm. I hear the wind rushing through the trees and the chirp of a songbird in my tree. It's all so beautiful . . .

MICRO-TRAILS. Each boy lines out his own micro-trail, a trail meant for crawling and peering. Although a special time is set aside the first evening for setting up the trails, the campers can also work on their trails during the odd moments. It's a good activity (for those not on the cook crew) to work on during meal preparation time, for example.

The first step is to collect ten sticks, six to twelve inches long (the firewood pile is declared off-limits!). Each stick is "tagged" with a small piece of orange "surveyors" tape, and each boy receives fifty feet of cord to use in marking off his trail. Everyone gets a pocket magnifying lens to help focus on some of the smaller features of the landscape.

Before they set out to make their trails, Jim conducts a tour of a sample micro-trail he has made. It's about fifty feet long with the sticks marking the special-interest "stops": a tiny fungus; a cicada "shell"; a fallen pine cone; a small spider web; some lichen growing on a little twig, and so forth. Each of the "stops" points out something to be looked at from ground level, close up, possibly with a magnifying lens. Jim suggests that a natural community is a lot like a pyramid and that little things are really more important than big things. "Little things are usually eaten by bigger things and it takes a lot of little things at the bottom of the pyramid to support the big things at the top! So it's those little things we don't notice that really count."

Before they begin, the boys get two "ground" rules: "You cannot use the bottoms of your feet on a trail, AND 'go slow as a slug!' " Then they set out, enthusiastically, to make their own trails. They enjoy sharing their discoveries. *It's amazing what you can find along just a few feet of ground, if you're looking. I'll take you on my trail if you'll take me on yours!*

They enjoy becoming "guides," giving a running commentary on their trail:

Here we have a little purple thing that you wouldn't usually see if you were just walking along. Take a look at the lacework on the underside of this leaf -- isn't it amazing? Here is a colony of moss - a whole colony growing right here! This is what we call a silver trumpet. It's only about a fourth of an inch tall, but see how neat it looks through this lens! Here is the entrance to an underground spider's nest. Look inside and see if you can see him. Down here, we have something of Mother Nature; this used to be a stick, but now it's becoming fertilizer. This plant has a disease. And here we have another helper of Mother Nature: this used to be a trunk, but now it's a place for all these little things to grow. A dragonfly helped me out here -- he left his wing; it's really delicate. And last, we come to the lichen lands. They almost look like coral, don't they?

In a space of just fifty feet, this boy saw things that he thought were interesting enough to share with his friends -- and things he, and they, would have missed if they hadn't been down on their knees, close up, and looking for "the little stuff."

SEEDS. The focus of the "seeds" technique is the immense variety of seeds in the world -- or even in just one little section of the world.

"What are some of the things people collect? . . ."

Stamps. Rocks. Coins. Insects. "Well, I collect something that probably none of you have ever collected, or even thought of collecting. I'm a seed collector. Here in this little can, I have some seeds I've just collected this morning. Take a look at these. Aren't they neat? Have you ever thought about how many kinds of seeds there are and just how MANY seeds? There must be thousands, millions, trillions of seeds, all kinds of seeds, with all sorts of ways of getting around. Floating. Flying. Here's a seed that hitch-hikes. I'd say that seeds with unique forms of transportation are more valuable to my collection. Some other things that I pay good 'prices' for are rarity, interesting coverings, and seeds with stories behind them. I want you to help me collect seeds here -- and you'll get a chance to sell them to me. First, I'd like to take you on a little tour. I call it 'The World of Seeds.' "

Into the lake we go, looking for examples of seeds. *Look, these are "drifters!" They drift into shore with the water.* Then to the forest, and finally to the bog. Jim points out a few kinds of seeds (the different kinds that are found in each community), but they've already got the idea. *Here's a neat kind. Oh, over here. Look, there goes one. I have some hitch-hikers already.* So he passes out flat, round film cans (about 3'' diameter), and the collecting begins. Half an hour is set aside for gathering, during which the leaders turn over the canoes to prepare a marketplace. Then, it's time for the big trading session -- one boy named it: *SEED '73!*

We'd thought ahead of time about what to use for money in our marketplace. What else? . . . . seeds! But special seeds that are edible -- peanuts! A seed for a seed seems a fair trade to the boys. Jim walks around, buying seeds for peanuts and giving each boy a lit-tle "seed money" to use in trading, too! Interest is high, both in the seeds and the "money", and the trading is fast and furious. *I've got a super seed that nobody else has! These are perfectly red seeds. I'll trade a hitch-hiker for a small cone and this red one. There's only one like this! I've got three cattails -- they're different stages; one's cotton candy.* They pull out their magnifying glasses to look more closely at the "special" seeds. *I'm opening up this pod to see what's inside -- a seed! In here's lots of seeds, probably hundreds; it came from a flower. This is where the flower was -- after it was pollinated, the flower withered off here.* The story makes the "pod-seed" more valuable to the collector -- two peanuts worth. *This is kind of like a barley seed, but it's from the bog. This one's a sparkler. You rub on it and the seeds pour out by the thousands! I've got sundew seeds. Here are my water seeds, fresh from the water grass. Fresh-picked water seeds! What would you give for four hitch-hikers? Four hitch-hikers is what ya get! These break open. These are all different colors. This one's rare -- it's red.*

When the trading is over, the merchants are asked to save two of their edible seeds -- to use as the price of admission to someone's micro-trail. Then, they begin "eating up the profits" -- some even decide to roast their "money" over the fire.

THE RAMBLE. We're sitting in a circle again, this time around a drum-shaped container of "ramble sticks" -- smooth branches about five feet long that make ideal walking sticks. They are notched and carved, each a little differently. Smooth and strong-looking, the sticks invite queries: *What are these for?*

"These will be your ramble sticks -- we're going on a ramble! We'll just wander around -- along the lakeshore, through the bog, into the forest -- sort of wherever the sticks lead us! We'll move along and we'll keep our senses alert for neat things along the way. When you

discover something that's interesting you can share it with all of us --
and we can bring some things back to look at again. And now, I'm
going to put on the 'magic coat' so we'll have everything we need.
You've got your sticks already. . .''

With the help of an 'assistant' Jim dons a safari-style jacket; but
this is his "Magic Coat of Many Pockets." Hidden in a seemingly infinite number of secret pockets are all sorts of special gadgets. He
reaches his hand into one large pocket and pulls out a set of cloth
bags and gives one to each boy in the circle.

"All kinds of neat stuff just seems to appear from this thing!
These bags are for each of you to use to put things in that you'd like
to look at later."

We set out, ramble sticks in hand, single file. Right away, the
boys begin pointing out their "finds." *Hey Jim! Look at this!* The ex-
clamation triggers a response, both from Jim and from his coat. One
time, he might draw from the depths of a pocket a small mirror to
direct a beam of light, so that everyone can spot a tiny fungus
growing on a nearby stump. Or he might pull out a sheet of white
paper to use as a backdrop behind a beautifully formed flower -- or a
black sheet to silhouette a spider's web. He has an atomizer to spray
water on things for smelling. There are small cardboard "sighting
tubes," -- looking through these, the boys can really focus in on
someone's discovery. And for the items to be carried back and viewed
at greater leisure, the coat holds a collection of small jars.

Discovery -- the *Wow! Look at this!* reaction -- is always rein-
forced with a gadget from the magic coat or with a sensory gimmick:
"What does it smell like?" or "Rub it against your cheek -- how does
that feel?" This is followed by still more discovery: *It* SMELLS *green.
It's fuzzy.*

After the ramble, we come back to camp and display the finds on
top of overturned canoes. Then, we go over to the sun again. "Now,
let's put up another strand of the web to represent these cool things
we found -- in the bog, along the lake, in the forest. Where does all of
the energy for all these things come from?" *THE SUN!* "Let's attach
some of these 'finds' right to the sun."

Finally, before supper, each boy carves another notch on the
stick he used. "Make your mark on the stick to represent the experience you had." With every ramble, the sticks pass from hand to
hand; each user adds to the carved design on the stick he carried.
The ramble sticks keep "growing" as the kids themselves grow
through their discoveries of a bit more of the natural world. The ramble sticks, in a way, help tell the story of that growth.

COCOONS. "Lie down on top of your sleeping bag and just relax. Close your eyes and let your whole body relax. Imagine that it's autumn; the leaves are just beginning to change color. You're no longer a human. You're a small caterpillar. As the leaves die and fall from the trees and the air begins to turn a little chilly, you start to prepare for something very special. It's time now this day for you to crawl up on a shrub and begin spinning a cocoon, your snug home for the winter.

"After you pull your cocoon up and over you, you might feel the winter wind blowing it around, making it sway and rock as it hangs from the branch. Finally, when Spring comes, you'll decide it's time to emerge. But you will have been inside so long that you don't know quite what to expect, so you come out very slowly, checking everything out. You emerge, not as a caterpillar, but as a butterfly. Once out, you might want to explore the changed world into which you've come."

Jim has been setting the tone for the "cocoon" experience. During Quiet Hour -- a traditional period after lunch when there's time to relax and unwind -- we take one camper at a time and let him role-play being a metamorphasizing butterfly. After the introduction, Jim starts the "caterpillar" on his way:

"Now it's time to crawl headfirst into your cocoon." The boy slithers into the bottom of his sleeping bag and the cocoon-carriers take their stations at each end of the poncho-and-pole stretcher upon which it has been resting. First, they turn the stretcher -- and its cocoon cargo -- around and around, and lift and rock it up and down to simulate the winter winds. Then, they head out to a spot in the forest to deposit the cocoon and depart, returning to camp to prepare another cocoon and waiting caterpillar.

The boy remains inside the sleeping bag until the sounds of footsteps have died away. As they carried him along, he had wondered, *What's happening? Where are they taking me?* Now, he wonders where he is, and wants to find out. He slowly, cautiously emerges from the security of his cocoon into the strangeness of an unknown place. First, he works his way around from the bottom of the bag until he is again "rightside up." Next, one hand cautiously gropes out, followed by another. A pair of eyes appear, blinking at the sudden exposure to light. A head pops out. The boy begins to crawl out, still on his belly, looking around:

At first I was just thinking 'where am I?' and it was weird. I stayed close to the bag so I wouldn't get lost. But I started wan-

dering farther and farther, sort of in circles, just exploring. I star-
ted to think of the trees and plants as being friendly -- instead of
being scared, I started to know that nothing would hurt me. I
started really exploring the plants. Then Jim came to see me and
we came back. It was cool.

The cocoon technique is another way of "making the familiar strange." By pretending to be something else for a while, the boys find that their perceptions of the environment change, too.

After the boys have tried emerging from cocoons into a new world, they go back to our sun and hook up another strand of colored yarn -- butterflies need sun, too, and their lives, perhaps much more than ours, are affected at a very basic level by the change of seasons, the different amount of light and heat. Another strand is added to the pattern that is growing -- a pattern that is beginning to look amazingly like a giant web.

GROKKING. To grok is to get to know -- to try to understand -- to experience. Jim demonstrated how to "grok" a tree.

"'Grokking' is a whole new way of looking at things, of getting to know something. In grokking, we don't just sense with our eyes and we don't just think with our heads. Grokking involves a special technique -- when we grok, we're going to see with all our senses. Instead of just thinking with our heads, we're going to think with our whole bodies. We'll pretend we're a different kind of creature from another planet. Our hands are very sensitive: rub the palms of your hands together for a minute." Their focus shifts to their hands as they rub; and the friction warms the palms and makes them more sensitive.

"When we grok, our hands are always flat, like this. Our fingers aren't able to grasp any more. You can pat or stroke with the palms or the backs of your hands. You can also touch very gently with your tongue, or brush with your nose or cheek or ear."

"You can use the other parts of your body, too, like your back or your stomach. You can take your shirts off if you wish. Compared with hands, the skin on other parts of your body is more sensitive. Feel the skin on the inside of your arm -- see how much more sensitive it is than your hand skin? You can hug the tree to grok, like this, and use that sensitive part of your skin."

"Usually when we try to sense something, our senses are mostly concentrated in our heads. Now, we're going to shift the focal point from the head to the whole body by masking off one sense. We'll put on these blindfolds and 'see' with our feet. Put your eyes on your big toes! And, so our feet will be able to see better, we'll take off our shoes and socks for a while."

We approached the rock -- blindfolded, barefooted, holding hands, walking carefully -- seeing with our feet. The "rock" is an unusual feature in this forest -- a glacier left it behind, and it stands alone as a monument to the ancient force of ice. Mosses, lichen, ferns and plants cover it, dripping down one side like a green waterfall. The uniqueness of this rock adds to the experience of grokking. The campers have never seen it before; when we stop a few feet in front of it, they still have no idea that it's there. Jim has them line up side by side, arms' lengths apart. "Now, just walk forward slowly until you come to something you might want to grok. When you stop, keep your feet planted."

When the initial contact is made, the grokking begins -- and the campers are both interested and perplexed by what the palms of their hands, their noses, ears, tongues and cheeks are telling them.

It's mossy. Over here, it's sort of smooth. It's a grave! Feels cold. Rough. It's bumpy. Hairy. Ooh, it's sharp here! There are holes in it. Here's a crack. Can we feel with our feet?

One foot still planted, this boy takes a "look" with his other.

Ooh, what is it?
It feels like a tree.
No. it feels like stone.
UUUUngh, it tastes TERRIBLE!
Is it a wall?
No, it's a tree. A big enormous old tree.
I have proof that it's a tree.
Nah, it's definitely a rock.
A ROCK!
Yeah, it even smells like a rock!
"Everybody move two steps to the right."
It's different here.
I feel little slits in it.
Here's a spider web.

Jim's voice is the "direction-finder" as they explore all around the rock. When he leads them back to their starting point, he asks, "Recognize anything?" *Hey, this is the exact place I started!* "How do you know?" *It feels the same.*

86

Then we retire to the spot where they left their shoes, to compare experiences. They put on their shoes, still blindfolded, and then take off the blindfolds. "Let's go back and see what that thing was."

They walk back eagerly to the rock. Their first reaction on seeing it is amazement: *I didn't think it was that big.* "How could this have gotten here -- how could it be moved without machines?"

I have an idea -- this could have been the shore, long ago.
It might have come from outer space!
Pushed up by water?
A glacier did it!
Hey, here's a chunk that came off!
This one was fitted right up here.
Look! some other pieces have fallen off.

"The glaciers were in this area maybe a million years ago, and they left behind this little gift. But what's happening to it now? Pieces are falling off -- what could do that?"

Water. In winter it freezes and just opens up.

"Then we could say that water is helping turn this rock into little pieces of rock. What else is here that might be helping break it up? Look at all these plants growing on it -- what are their roots doing to it? What's happening to the rock?"

The plants are turning it into soil, someday it will just be soil.

"And then other plants can grow in the soil. This rock, that the glacier left a long, long, time ago, will be helping plants grow a long, long time from now!"

"See if you can find your original spot along the rock."
Here's mine!
Mine was by this crack.
I think this is where I was.

THE SHARING CAMPFIRE. Fire. It crackles, and people sit in a circle around it -- as people have probably done since the first controlled spark touched off civilization. Faces glow in the light of the flame . . . people draw closer together, seeking from the fire and from each other -- warmth, safety, a refuge from the dark.

Camping out NEEDS a fire, not only for cooking, but for this ritual of sitting around a fire at the close of day, telling stories, singing songs and seeing, in the flickering light, dreams. In these ways, our sharing campfire is like all campfires. In another way, it is very different. After the stories are told and the marshmallows are toasted, Jim begins. His voice drifts quietly across the flame:

"Let's all close our eyes for a couple of minutes and listen to the sounds of night in this place -- the waves on the shore, the wind in the trees, the crackle of the fire . . ."

The mood of the "fire-brothers" becomes hushed, attentive to nature's voices, and expectant.

"Now I'm going to pass around a very special 'magic kettle.' I'm holding it now. It's about twenty inches across, and the outside is all charred black from the soot of many, many fires like this one. It is special because, although you can't see it with your eyes, you can put things into it and take things from it. I'm going to pass it around, and when it comes to you, put in something you have that you think would help others be more aware of the natural environment. And then, using your other hand, take from the magic kettle some quality, or ability that you would like to have but don't have now - one that would increase YOUR OWN awareness of the natural world. . ."

We sit with eyes closed and heads slightly bowed as the kettle passes from hand to hand, around the circle. It grows with each thing we put in it, yet it holds more than we can possibly take from it. Each person quietly states his gift to the kettle and his wish from it!

I'd like to put in the idea that water's not really everywhere -- that we should spare it; and I'd like to take out being around fish a lot more than I am now.

I'd like to put in the kettle being aware of more sounds, like we just did -- the water and the shore, the trees, the wind, the crackling of the fire and everything. I'd like to take out being in the woods a lot more than I am in the city.

I'd like to put in the awareness I have when I'm on canoe trips and cooking and camping. I'd like to take out -- to be more aware of little things, to be more comfortable and to be more aware of what I'm doing.

I'd like to put in the kettle the awareness of night ·and how it's different from day -- and the two things are two different worlds, and they're completely separate. And it's like a new world coming in at night. And I'd like to take out the awareness of life. Why was there ever life? What's the meaning of life? What's the point?

I'd like to put in the kettle an awareness of how many trees we chop down and wood that we use. And I'd like to take out of the kettle just to sit in the woods by myself and listen to the sounds and watch wildlife pass.

I have something else to put in, besides what I did already.

I'd like to put in the kettle being out here, sitting at this campfire -- it's a lot better than being in the cabin, doing nothing. It's better to be doing stuff like telling this and listening to the sounds that you can hear and -- you could have a little chat with a tree if you wanted to! It's a lot better being outdoors than indoors, especially at night.

I'd like to put in the awareness, also, that what we're burning in this fire right now is wood, and wood comes from trees. What makes trees grow is water, the air, the light, and all that stuff that's going into it. And it's all going up in flames right before our eyes.

Wow! It's different to watch a fire and think about what it really is.

That kettle is really cool!

FOXES AND RABBITS. This is a game that can be played during any open time slot. Here are the ground rules:

Divide the group into "foxes," "rabbits," and "leaves." (With a group of ten, have 4 rabbits, 3 leaves, and 3 foxes.)

Rabbits have tails (pieces of cloth to stick in back pockets).

Foxes form a large circle with rabbits inside, leaves outside.

When the signal is given, rabbits must try to get (tag) leaves; foxes try to get rabbits by pulling tails; leaves are immobile.

Rabbits are "safe" when frozen in crouching position. Rabbits may not move or get leaves without standing up. And rabbits must get food within each round or they die and become leaves.

When a fox catches a rabbit, the rabbit becomes a fox; but if the fox fails to catch a rabbit within the round, he "dies" and becomes a leaf. If the rabbit fails to get food, he dies and becomes a leaf, too. When the rabbit gets food, the food becomes a rabbit.

If there are too many rabbits, there isn't enough food, so some of the rabbits die and become food; plus, it is easier for the foxes to get rabbits, so some rabbits may become foxes. If there are too many foxes, they can't all get rabbits, so some die and become food. Which means that it's easier for rabbits to get food, so there will be more rabbits, so that the foxes can get food again!

There is one problem -- the possibility that everyone ends up as a leaf. This can be used as an example of overpopulation, but it is better to establish one more ground rule: Although foxes may only get one rabbit in each round, rabbits may get more than one leaf.

The game could, theoretically, be endless, so set ahead of time a specified number of rounds, as well as the length of each. Consider posting the resulting numbers at the end of each round on a slateboard, to be used for a discussion of numbers and balance after the game.

INTERVIEWS. Have the campers choose some specific natural object and say: I'm a seed (pebble, piece of bark, leaf, flower . . . .); interview me. Then ask them questions ABOUT what they are. Ask: Where have you spent most of your life? What is your favorite food? Are you afraid of anything? Do you like your neighbors? Do you like the rain? What is your favorite season? Do you like people to touch you? Whom do you depend on? Do you interact with things that live by you? Do you have any patterns in the way you live? After having been interviewed by the leader a few times, the group may want to pair up and play the interview game with each other.

E.P.'S. A productive variation of the interview technique is where the leader plays the role of an environmental problem. Taking up a position in the middle of a circle of campers, the leader announces "I am a man-made environmental problem (e.p.) on this site. I affect each one of you. What am I?" After identifying the problem, the real task is to trace the problem to each of the participants. And it's a two-way street: how the problem affects the camper and how the camper affects the problem!

MAGIC RAFT. Drift silently on rubber rafts in the calm waters of morning or evening. Just float on the surface of the water, first gazing upward, then turning over and with a face mask peer into the water.

HOMES. In the first round, ask each of the participants to choose a native, ground-dwelling animal which he would like to become. Everyone announces his choice to the group. Then, on signal, they all rush out to find something their animal would use. It could be food, nest materials, plaything -- ANYTHING the individual can connect to the animal he is role-playing. Upon returning, everyone explains and shares his choice.

In the second and longest round, send each "animal" out to find a home. (He can make himself a new home from scratch, or adopt a vacant structure!) Plenty of time should be given to construction efforts as the leader makes the rounds of the new "community," discussing decisions as to location, materials, necessities, comforts, etc. Later, everyone can provide a tour of his new home.

NOTHING LIVES ALONE. Place a natural object in the middle of the group's circle, and ask them to imagine what would ordinarily "fill in" the spaces around it. Begin with easy items (pine cone, beach pebble, snail shell), and then produce something more difficult -- like a certain type of bird's feather. What would be right next to it? What would be right underneath it? Directly above it? Further away, but still around it? Have each participant take a turn. Build layers, or circles, out from that focal point, and finally you have a community. Now produce an object brought in from a different community. Ask the same questions of this object and try to reconstruct this community which is out of sensory contact. Then return to another object from the immediate area and try again to construct the community with ever widening circles which may touch other neighboring communities. What lives in one's community? What associations are there in overlapping communities?

LASSOING AN ANT. Appear at the community center with a fairly good sized piece of rope. Quietly, but with apparent concentration, begin fashioning and testing a large lasso loop. To the inevitable questions, reply that you are going to "lasso an ant!" Lead your group of doubters off to a nearby clearing and with great enthusiasm cast your loop. Almost without fail a "close inspection" of the loop will turn up at least one ant. (They're slippery little fellows though so don't be too chagrined if you miss once in a while!) That inspection, by the way, can lead to all sorts of other challenges -- like counting and categorizing all the different sorts of life found within the loop.

RAINTREE. Need a good rainy day activity? Don't hole up in your tents. Get everyone in a poncho and head for the edge of the marsh. You can all become trees soaking in the rain! Take OFF your hoods, hold your bare arms OUTSIDE your poncho, and root your sneakers to the ground! Let the rain wash over your face like the rivulets on leaves, let the wind push you to and fro like the swaying trunks of the trees. After a few minutes, you'll actually be able to see through the water in your eyes, your arms will sag like rain-drenched boughs, and your feet will grip the earth against the gusts of wind blowing across the open spaces. It's an exhilarating experience; a role-playing idea that will place you in direct contact with the elements.

CAMOUFLAGE GAME. Scatter dozens of colored toothpicks (equal numbers of red, yellow, green, brown) over a separate area of the ground ahead of time. Prepare for the action by explaining to the campers that camouflage plays an important role in adaptation (everything grows to fit where and how it lives). Many plants and animals have adapted to the place where they live in the protective coloration which helps hide them from predators. Then lead the group to their "hunting grounds" where everyone collects as many toothpicks as possible in one minute. Sort the toothpicks collected into colored piles and tally how many of each color were retrieved. The results set the stage for a discussion of adaptive traits (both form and color), and hopefully raise questions about the effect such patterns play upon our perception. (Another line of discussion can deal with plants and animals which use colors to attract or distract others. Don't forget to include man!)

The Environmental Study Station is a way of extending the Acclimatizing approach into what was once a rather ordinary campout. There is a double thrust at the ESS -- two major goals which we hope to accomplish. First, it serves as an introduction to outdoor living for those who have never been camping -- AND for those who have "camped" without ever really living in the out-of-doors! Secondly, and emphatically, the experience further heightens sensory and conceptual awareness -- to use living *in* the natural environment as an opportunity for becoming more involved *with* it.

"Campouts" signify to most of us an organized chaos, at best, of tents, equipment, duffles, burnt food, and bright faces around a smoky fire, perhaps a hike or two -- and many missed opportunities. If we are fortunate, our own memories of early campouts are good, and now we enjoy camping. The unlucky ones, however, have long since been so "turned off" by a misguided first exposure that they will never willingly venture forth into the wilderness. If they ever do "camp" again, it will be within the security and confinement of a fully-equipped motor home! And they will have missed so much. In this day when natural awareness is so vital and involvement so sought-after, it borders on the criminal to have the results of that first experiment so entirely dependent upon unknowns. Can we afford to leave it to chance, when it means the difference between a sense of joy in living with nature and a bundle of fears, prejudices, and alibis? In our ACC work we hoped to come up with a viable alternative to "chance" -- an experience in which the mechanics would be worked out and the program designed for total involvement. Learning to live with nature -- and living with nature in order to learn: these are what we set out to do at the ESS.

There is one crucial concept at the core of the Environmental Study Station format, an idea which meshes easily with both the outdoor living and the natural awareness aspects of the plan. That concept is the Web of Life -- the interrelatedness of all things. When we live in the out-of-doors, we are more aware of our place in nature as well as of the interdependence of all life. Camping, we work together as a community and are aware of the interactions among members of the group. We are aware of our needs and how they are supplied. And we have a chance to observe, for three days, how the Web of Life is woven all around us. For this, we have special techniques, just as we have special mechanics for the business of living outdoors. The techniques stimulate-encourage-actuate involvement. The mechanics keep everything going smoothly -- eating, cleaning, sleeping, rising -- so that there's more time for other things. Like grokking a rock. Making micro-trails. Rambling. And getting into seeds.

general   • this is a two and one-half day experience

>> day one: arrive-set up camp
>>> the model
>>> the sun
>>> magic spots
>>> begin work on micro-trails
>>> grokking

>> day two: morning - seeds
>>> quiet hour - cocoons
>>> afternoon - ramble
>>> evening - sharing campfire

>> day three: pack and leave

• all of the special equipment is carried in the "magic bag," a large duffle:

>> materials for the model
>> sheet and ropes for the sun; yarn strands
>> magnifying lenses and day-glo tape
>> ramble sticks
>> magic coat
>> blindfolds
>> seed cans
>> rabbit tails
>> clipboard and felt-tip pens

• before going on an Environmental Study Station trip, the campers should have experienced a six-hour *Acclimatization* program and a six-hour program of basic campcraft skills.

• have a packing list and adhere to it. Omit comic books, radios, bubble gum.

• campers should pack a set of "swamp clothes" -- long pants, long-sleeved shirt, tennis shoes, extra socks.

• trippers should check that everyone has packed all items on the list: especially raingear, warm clothing, and swamp clothes.

• anybody can clean dishes. Let the campers do the cooking while your counselors do the washing! Remember: it's learning by doing.

• appoint a "pollution control agent" every day. One of his jobs is to make sure hands are washed in the basin, not the lake -- no soap in the lake -- and that everything is taken out that was taken in.

every aspect of the camping experience can be used as an environmental education opportunity. One example that's very easy is MEALS. Talk about where the food comes from: the names we use for food so often fail to really describe it. Bread is really seeds, crushed and baked. The pancakes are made from seeds, too. The syrup is either tree sap or it comes from a sweet root. Meat comes from animals, which eat plants. (you might even see a hamburger as a form of grass!) We post our daily fare on a slateboard, calling the items by their actual names. For example:

roast pig
boiled orange roots
baked ground seeds and cow's milk
mashed fruit pulp

model

●the "community" analogy really begins before departing for the site. At the put-in point, hand a paddle to each camper. Have the group form a circle with each camper placing the blade of his paddle in the center. Lay the paddles down and sit at the perimeter of the spokes. Focus on how the paddles are all touching each other in a way that connects everyone together. Use an analogy to a bee hive: each bee has its job. If all work together, the needs of the community will be fulfilled and all will be well. "As the trip progresses, we'll be discovering the needs that we have and we'll decide together how to fulfill them."

●our first need is to put the gear into the canoes. We use a fire brigade method, forming a line to "pass, don't throw" everything down to one of the leaders, who helps load the gear and equalize it in each canoe.

●a second need is cooperation among paddlers. You will have to remind them of this!

●setting up the model is followed by a tour, where the ground rules can be reiterated and questions can be answered. Suggest choice tent locations, point out where life jackets will be hung, the wash-up area, and location of the litter bag and latrine. Also highlight some of the natural features of the area; point out where birch bark has been peeled, and its ugly consequences; and suggest that they "use the route, not the roots" by staying on paths instead of trampling plants. Use a "pointing" stick; ham it up -- play the tour-guide role!

●the community model can be extended even further for older groups, with a three-phase plan. First, the day before the planned departure, assemble the group around a huge mound of equipment (tents and gear) covered by a tarp. Tell them that at the Environmental Study Station, you'll provide the program, but they have to figure out how they're going to live -- WHAT to take and HOW to take it. You're there to make suggestions and to make sure everything goes smoothly, but they have to make the decisions. Phase II begins at the put-in point, when they decide who goes in what canoe, who paddles, and what equipment each canoe will carry. The third phase, at the site, is for setting up the community itself -- who sleeps in what tent, who cooks first, etc. The ground rules still hold, however.

sun

●the sun is attached to the rope frame by short elasticized hook lines, so that it is tightly stretched. The rope frame is made from one long piece of rope tied to form a square with four corner ropes used to attach it to the tree. (Have another rope already strung up between two trees so that the two top corner ropes of the frame can be swung over this line, for quicker hoisting.)

●the "strands" are made from brightly colored rug yarn. Each strand is a series of large, chain-like loops, made by pulling the yarn through one loop to form another -- like crocheting. When the strands are put up, attach them to the middle of the sun and to an outside edge, then weave others around, starting at the center and working out. The effect is similar to a large multi-colored spider web -- the web of life.

●tie the sun into other events by putting up a strand after each activity. And encourage people to stick their "finds" into the loops of a strand.

●hold community meetings in front of the sun, using it as a backdrop. Set up the seed market in front of it, too.

magic spots   ●in setting up the location of "magic" spots it is important that everyone is spread out enough so that each feels secluded. One way to do this is to take the group out yourself and point out general areas as you drop each one off.

●these are multiple-use places. Suggest good times for people to go off to their spots -- like right after a meal or before reveille. Suggest that individuals may want to check out a clipboard and felt-tip pen to use for writing or sketching. You may even want to suggest that perhaps someone needs some time to himself, particularly after a verbal scrap. However, don't *send* anyone to their "spot" -- don't mention it by name, just say that you would like for the camper to spend some time alone.

micro-trail   ●have campers collect the sticks without telling them what they're for; keep the end result a surprise until you take them on the sample tour. (And have them hide their sticks, until ready to use them.)

●purchase inexpensive plastic hand lenses. Drill holes in the handles and loop a two-foot length of cord through so they can be worn around the neck and hung up at night. This prevents both loss and breakage. An added touch -- labeling each lens with a camper's name -- makes identifying the "lost and found" much easier as well as personalizing them.

●when you're setting up the demonstration trail, take time to look for different types of "little stuff" so that they'll think of having a wide variety, too. Introduce the trail with a group input, perhaps a storyline (like entering an ant's community), but take the campers along it in smaller groups, a pair at a time. Remember: you only crawl on a micro-trail.

●provide enough cord -- 50 ft. apiece -- so each "trail-blazer" can mark his claim; this prevents needless trampling. You may want to mark off the entire construction area as the campers will become quite possessive about their own territories. Use the opportunity to point up how other animals mark their boundaries.

• the admission price for the micro-trail -- to visit someone else's -- is one peanut. These are saved from the "seed market." (A survey done in the National Parks revealed that more people visit a park that charges admission than one that is free -- the logic perhaps being that if it costs something to get in, it must be good.)

seeds

• swamp clothes are worn for the "world of seeds" tour. During the tour be sure to make the point that different types of seeds are found in different communities.

• use the magnifying lens like a jeweler would -- right up in front of the eye.

• use empty micro-film cans for seed cans. These are good because they fit in a pocket, they close tightly, and can be easily obtained.

• set aside half an hour for gathering, then re-group.

• to set up the "market," arrange four canoes in a square. The leader (buyer) operates from the center of the square. Each camper sets up a "booth" or display on a canoe, from the outside of the square. (Encourage the campers to include decorations and special exhibits for their seeds.)

• encourage trading between displayers.

• go around the square, talking with each camper for a few minutes about his collection and making some initial trades. Run through the circuit twice, then tell them that this will be the last round. Be sure no one is slighted when "buying" seeds.

• when "buying," shake seeds to listen to them, ask the displayer about the color and shape of the seed, its origin. Look at it through your lens. Encourage them to examine the seeds carefully by doing so yourself.

• have a special pouch to carry the "seed money" in.

• have a collection of little jars--or a collecting belt of vials--to put the seeds in when you "buy" them from the displayers; as you put more seeds in, they begin to create patterns inside the jars; another focal point!

• special note: for those concerned that this seed market seems more like a lesson in "micro-economics" than anything else, don't be. The young merchants are not at all adverse to eating up the profits!

ramble

• change into swamp clothes before beginning the ramble.

• the ramble is discovery-oriented and loose. The group stays together, though, and the leader reinforces individual discoveries, calling them to the attention of the group.

97

- the ramble should go through several communities: the marsh, the forest, and the lakeshore.

- have each camper attach his "neatest" item to the sun by putting it into a loop of one of the strands.

- the ramble takes an hour or slightly longer.

- the cloth (re-usable) bags are about the size of a 5-lb. flour sack.

- review the techniques for group control outlined in *Acclimatization*.

- be spontaneous in the direction the group wants to go (wandering).

- collect cloth bags and ramble sticks (after new notches have been carved) -- they should be returned to the magic bag.

cocoon

- each camper is called individually from his tent for the cocoon experience. (It may be done in two shifts: five during quiet hour, and five later.) The stretcher is made with a poncho and two poles -- first-aid style.

- this technique requires two fairly husky "cocoon-carriers" -- or have the campers who aren't participating at the time help carry stretchers for the others.

- take the cocoon to an area of the forest which the camper will not recognize immediately, to strengthen the idea of emergence into a new world.

- have the camper remove his shoes before entering his cocoon, and tie the shoes onto the zipper of the bag.

- the lifting, rocking and dipping both simulates the winter winds and loosens the camper's sense of direction.

- be sure to explain the process of emergence -- it should proceed SLOWLY, CAREFULLY, after the footsteps have died away.

- allow about fifteen minutes for the emergence and exploration. Instruct the campers to return to camp if they have figured out where they are, otherwise to remain there and you'll pick them up.

- place the cocoons so the campers are spread out enough to prevent distracting each other. If possible, take them out in different directions from the campsite.

- use a serious, quiet tone; be sure there are no undue fears.

- the interior of a sleeping bag will get hot -- it may take some only about five minutes to emerge. Try to avoid using extremely heavy bags. If you're in an area with a very hot climate, consider an alternative like a special bag made from only one layer of dark cloth.

grokking
- try grokking rocks, trees, a big stump, or the ground itself (grok the earth!).

- remember the three p's of grokking: Patting Prevents Picking. We don't pluck, pull, or tear apart while we're grokking -- it is *touching without breaking*.

- going barefoot discourages climbing, which if not dangerous, is at least destructive to the community that lives upon the rock.

- there is a tendency to move -- remind everyone that to grok, you plant your feet; they are rooted to the ground.

- to explore around the rock, talk them through it; your voice is the direction-finder and a reassurance as well as a control.

- for the sharing, hold hands to form a circle, and let each person in turn describe what he felt while grokking. Leave the blindfolds on for this, so they don't start looking around for the rock and get distracted.

- go back to the rock for another look -- to see the difference between what was felt and what is seen, and to get the visual impact. It's also a good time to hit the concepts: land formation, soil formation, plant succession.

- when we return to the rock, we still discourage climbing by focusing on how delicate the plants are and how beautiful they are, growing from the rock.

sharing campfire
- eating, singing, and active games might come at the beginning of this campfire, but things slow down and become more low-keyed toward the end. Tell a natural history story to relax the tone before beginning the sharing portion.

- closing of eyes helps set the tone for quiet and seriousness.

- each participant should begin by *repeating* the opening phrase, then filling in his own thoughts. (Bowing heads minimizes self-consciousness -- instruct them to tap the person on the shoulder as they pass the kettle on.)

- keep the fire small. Assign one fire tender so that chore doesn't become distracting. Re-emphasize that we don't play with fire.

- have a quiet, low-keyed ending for the campfire. (Sing taps, read a poem, etc.)

options
- these techniques can be substituted for those in the regular program, added to those already included, or used as foul weather alternatives.

AN ENVIRONMENTAL STUDY TRAIL

This is going to be fun!
Can we write pictures down of what it is?
Four needs of life:
a time for every need, and a need for every time.
This is how much rain fell! It's just a little tad under one inch.
How much is in this one?
The one in the clearing should have more!
This is my own symbol for water.
I used a man for the animal. Here's the plant giving off oxygen and here's the man breathing it.
It's orange -- the paper is orange. Let's see . . . strongly acid.
It was that tree -- you wouldn't have noticed that if you just walked by it.
It took the stuff from the soil and now it's giving it back.
It's nourishing the plants!

As we walk toward the trailhead that marks the beginning of the Environmental Study Trail, someone calls out: "Hey, where are you guys going? Is this some kind of an expedition?"

It IS some kind of an expedition -- we're going to try out a newly developed trail. The Environmental Study Trail is different from most trails; it's designed for the campers who are interested in pursuing a little further some of the concepts they learned in *Acclimatization.* Each of the campers has a clipboard, a pencil, and a booklet that is written with a programmed learning format. They know something about what they're going to do: read the booklet as they go, filling in the blank spaces when they occur, and experimenting with various data-gathering devices at different stations. The trail has twenty such stations, and for each, there is a concept-oriented reading, an experiment of sorts to perform, and a touch of magic.

The first stop--to introduce the trail -- is called the "magic mountain." A fallen tree, its roots exposed, is supporting moss, lichen, small plants, and spiders.

It really is like a miniature forest. It's sort of like its own little world.

After peering at this "world of the fallen tree," the boys walk down the trail. They stop at the second post. The note on the wooden box reads: "Inside this box are the four basic needs of all life. Can you name them?" They try, and then open the box. Inside, they find a flask of water, a saucer of soil, and a sign that says, "Here are two of them. One other was here all the time, and the fourth entered when you opened the box."

Air was always there.

And when we opened it, sunlight came in!

Light, air, water, and soil are the four needs of life -- this is one of the key concepts emphasized throughout the trail. There are five key concept strands: needs, cycles, conditions, forms, changes.

And so it goes. From here, we continue down the trail which takes us to the marsh, along the lakeshore, and through a changing forest landscape. The boys read, take temperatures, check wind speeds, measure, and record -- and touch and taste and smell and feel and see. They work with the programmed learning booklet, and they find it surprisingly easy to remember the key words.

You use the same words a lot!

They also find the data gathering fun and the natural world a little more fascinating, even, than it was before. The format and the length of the trail makes it obvious that this is not equally exciting for everyone. Some people like the approach, and some don't. For the boys who are looking for a way of learning more about their environment and are willing to spend an afternoon to do it, however, the

Environmental Study Trail has a lot to offer. As one of the boys put it, "The whole thing was to be interesting, and to learn, too." And learning does happen:

There's no wind here -- it's all over the tops of the trees.

Coming in through here it's only 2 miles an hour.

It's a lot drier here--more solid, sandier. Warmer, a bit.

This isn't adapted to living here!

That's what happened to the dinosaurs. Their conditions for life changed, but they couldn't adapt!

It just repeats itself.

Here's my little box of life: water is on my hand; air was always there; light, when I opened it; this little clump of soil; and this plant from the marsh, for food.

STATION ONE. Look very closely at this miniature world of the fallen tree. It is a "magic mountain." If you come really close and peer at it, you can see that it is a tiny community -- a small example of the life that is all around you. It is magical because, for this mountain, you can be a giant. Blow gently on the "trees" of the magic mountain to create the wind for this little world. Stand in front of it and cast your shadow over the community like a cloud passing in front of the sun. A few tiny drops of water is a rain-storm here; the micro-community has a micro-climate. As you take this trail, notice how the forces of wind, sun, and rain affect the larger communities along the Nakomis shore. As you walk, stop at the numbered posts to read the passages about some of the visible and invisible forces at work in each place. Filling in the blanks as you read will help you become more familiar with some key concepts about the natural world. You will also be gathering data which you can use to discover some of the things that in-fluence your environment and how all of them are related. You will see how the NEEDS of life work in CYCLES, how those cycles set the CONDITIONS for life, and how the FORMS of life have made CHANGES to meet those conditions.

Let the magical beauty of this mountain help you see the larger communities ahead. They, too, have magic. Use your SENSES . . . see clearly . . . listen attentively . . . touch gently.

STATION TWO.

Read the note on the box. What are the four basic NEEDS of life? Record them

here: _____, _____, _____, and _____.

We call light, air, water and soil the four basic NEEDS of life because without them life as we know it could not exist. The NEEDS of life are the four things that make life on earth possible. Plants use the four basic _____ of life to produce food. Green plants contain green FOOD-MAKING parts which give them their color. All GREEN plants have these _____ - _____ parts. Most living things which contain food-making parts are _____-colored. These food-making parts allow plants to change LIGHT energy from the sun into a type of energy they can use for growth and store as food. To do this, they also need AIR; WATER; and SOIL. The basic needs for plant life, then, are _____, _____, _____, and _____.

STATION THREE. WATER is one of the four basic needs of life. Tiny drops of WATER are carried in the air. The tiny drops of WATER in the air come from the EVAPORATION of water from the surface of the earth. Lakes, oceans, rivers, soil, plants and animals all lose water to the air through _____ from their surfaces.

Hang one of the paper towels on the frame in the sun and one in the shade.

Which do you think will dry faster? (The towels will dry as the water in them

EVAPORATES into the air.) Check on the way back to see what has happened;

then return the towels to their box.

The water that has evaporated from the surface of the earth collects in the air as clouds. When there are enough of the small drops of water in the clouds and they are close enough together, the small drops join to become larger drops. This is called CON-DENSATION. The larger drops might fall as RAIN -- or, if it is cold enough in the clouds, as snow, sleet, or hail. PRECIPITATION is the way water returns to the earth from the air. RAIN, snow, sleet and hail are all types of _____. Most of the precipitation that falls here in the summer is the type called _____ (or TP dew!).

Record the total amount of precipitation here for the summer: _____in-

ches. How much do you think will be here by the end of camp?

You can see that water is always moving. It always goes away, and it always comes back. This happens over and over again, so we say that water moves in a CYCLE. A _____ is something that happens over and over again.

EVAPORATION, CONDENSATION, and PRECIPITATION are important parts of the water cycle. Water leaves the surfaces of the earth by _____, collects in clouds through _____, and returns to earth as _____, making a complete and continuous CYCLE. The water cycle is the largest PHYSICAL action on earth. As you stand here, the water is leaving the lake and going into the air. On a warm, windy day, the lake may lose 1/2 to 3/4 inch of water. It may lose as much as 20-22 inches of water in one month! The lake doesn't dry up, though, because water returns as precipitation or rain.

STATION FOUR. So far, you have seen that one of the needs of all life is water. Then, at the last stop, you found that water moves in a _____ of life -- from the earth to the sky and from the sky back to the earth. Part of this water goes through the plant and animal life of the earth. The AMOUNT and TYPE of water for any animal or plant in the CYCLE helps to make up its CONDITIONS for life. The amount and type of any of the four needs of life help set the conditions for life in an area.

The amount of PRECIPITATION in an area determines the kinds of plants that can grow there. Plants that need very little WATER have grown to FIT (or have ADAPTED to) dry areas. Those that need a great deal of water are _____ to areas of greater rainfall -- they have grown to fit the areas that have more water.

Does the same amount of rain reach the earth in the forest as in the clearing?

Record the amount of water in each of the rain gauges. Forest: _____ inches;

clearing: _____ inches. Can you explain this? Are the plants that are growing in

the two places the same?

A difference in the amount of one of the needs of life can make a big difference in the FORMS of life that can develop in any area. A FORM of life is the way a plant or animal grows to fit its CONDITIONS for life. Different plants have ADAPTED to the same conditions for life in different ways; some cannot adapt at all to certain conditions for life, so they cannot live where those conditions exist. A pine tree cannot live in a desert, and a cactus can't grow here! Different forms of plant life are _____ to areas with different amounts of rainfall. Many plants grow more during a wet summer than during a dry summer; these plants do better when there is more water. Look at the tree stumps here. Because the tree grows a new layer each year, its "rings" can tell you in which summers there was more rain. Wide rings - wet summers; thin rings - dry summers.

How old were these three trees? _____ years; _____ years; _____ years.

In what year did they grow the most? _____.

STATION FIVE. Look around you. There are a lot of things here that are breathing. Can you tell which ones? Take several deep breaths at this point. Listen to the sound of your breathing. Imagine what it would sound like if you could hear the breathing of all these plants and animals.

Why do all plants and animals breathe? We already know that all life NEEDS air, but why is it so important? The air has many parts called gases. In the beginning, most of the earth's air was made up of the gas called "carbon dioxide." There wasn't much oxygen in the air--and there weren't any animals living then, either. A green plant uses water, "carbon dioxide" gas from the air, and LIGHT energy to make food and give off oxygen. Entering the green plants' leaves, _____ energy from the sun splits the water in the leaves into two gases: hydrogen and oxygen. Then, the CARBON DIOXIDE gas from the air combines with the HYDROGEN from the water to form a CARBO-HYDRATE particle (like sugar) -- or what we call FOOD. (You can tell from the name of the carbo-hydrate particle that it is made of carbon and hydrogen!) All the extra OXYGEN goes into the air. This is the largest CHEMICAL action on earth!

In brief, in the plant, the _____ dioxide from the air and the gases from the water combine with the light energy to store carbo-hydrates (food) and give off extra _____ to the air.

Draw a picture diagram showing how a plant uses the NEEDS of life to make food. (6 parts water + 6 parts carbon dioxide + light energy = 1 part "food" + 6 parts oxygen)

Do you see now that once green plants started taking in _____ dioxide from the air and giving off _____, there was more and more oxygen and less and less carbon dioxide? Turn and look at the forest here. One acre of this forest takes in about 2,000 pounds of carbon dioxide each year and gives off about 1,500 pounds of oxygen. So today there isn't much carbon dioxide in the air -- but there is a lot of carbon stored in the plants as carbo-hydrates!

Animals take in air, but unlike the plants, the animals can't use the carbon dioxide to make food. However, the animals CAN use the oxygen in the air. Remember what the plant did to make food? It took in air, water and light. In the end, it stored carbo-hydrates and gave off oxygen to the air. Well, the animal eats *that* food and breathes *that* oxygen. In the animal, the oxygen combines with the carbo-hydrate to RELEASE energy and give off extra water and carbon dioxide (and store some of the carbo-hydrates, too!)

Do you see how the animal's breathing is just the opposite of the plant's breathing? Breathe on the mirror here to see one of the things given off when an animal breathes. Draw a diagram below which shows the relationship between a plant's breathing and that of an animal.

STATION SIX. You have already seen that water is always moving. The air is always moving, too. WIND is air in motion.

Pause and listen to the wind for a moment.

Plants in a windy area (where there is air in motion) must be able to bend with the wind or be strong enough to withstand its pushing. Whatever lives in an area must be adapted to the CONDITIONS for life in that area. In a windy area, they must be adapted to the AMOUNT and TYPE of one of the basic needs of life -- air. The _____ and _____ of each of the basic needs of life helps make up the conditions for life in any area.

The wind vane points to the direction from which the wind (air in motion) is coming. Record the direction and speed: from the _____ at _____ m.p.h.

The wind isn't just air, though. As you have seen, the wind carries with it drops of _____ which sometimes collect in clouds and fall as precipitation. Besides water, the wind can carry dust, seeds and leaves. The wind here usually comes from across the open space of the lake. The things the wind brings here help determine the CON-DITIONS for life here, and the plants that live here must be adapted to those _____ for life. The wind itself is a condition for life, since it can affect this area in a forceful way. When the _____ is strong, it can knock over trees. Wind can be blocked off by trees in some places. The trees shelter some areas from the push of the wind and block out the things it carries. The marsh here is open -- it isn't sheltered. Why is this a marsh? The small sheltered cove by the last stop is not a marsh, because it is protected from the wind. Here, the wind is not blocked off. In the spring, the wind pushes the ice to shore and pushes soil with it to form sand bars and "ridges." These ridges separate the marsh here from the lake. Where there are no ridges pushed up by ice and _____, there is no marsh. The sheltered area is not a marsh, then, because it is protected from the wind and therefore doesn't have ridges to separate it from the lake.

Look at the two pinwheels. Where does the wind have more "push"--in the open or where there are trees?

STATION SEVEN. The four basic _____ of life (light, air, water and soil) exist in different amounts and types in different areas. The amount and type of each of the basic needs make up the _____ for life in any area. TEMPERATURE is the amount of heat in something. The sun's light energy gives us heat -- heat is really a type of light energy. Certain rays of the sun are changed to heat when they pass through the earth's air or strike its surface. You already know that plants store light energy from the sun. Fire is like a piece of the sun. When something burns, it gives off heat and light because the stored energy inside it is being released.

Everything has a temperature. To measure the amount of heat in something, you can take its _____ with a thermometer. The amount of heat in your body is your temperature. People usually have a temperature of about 98°. Why do some things feel cold to you? If something is cold, it has a lower _____ than you do. Does the soil here have a lower temperature than you do? To find out you can take its temperature with the thermometer. What about the air? or the water?

Record the temperature of the following: air _____°; water _____°; soil

_____°. Which one is warmer?

Can you explain why?

Everything has a heat temperature at which it can live. If the amount of _____ is too little for a plant, it can't grow, but if the amount of heat is too great, the plant can't grow, either. It has grown to fit (or has ADAPTED to) living only at certain temperatures. For example, these marsh plants grow here because they are _____ to the CONDITIONS for life here. Temperature is one of the important conditions for life.

Is the temperature of the ground the same everywhere? Using the flat back of your hand, feel the temperature of the boardwalk; reach underneath the boardwalk and feel the temperature there. Then put your hand on a sunny spot beside the boardwalk. Can your hand tell the differences in the temperatures of these areas?

STATION EIGHT. At the stop back in the forest you found that there wasn't much carbon dioxide in the earth's air. In fact, over 3/4 of the air is made up of a gas called "nitrogen." Nitrogen is a necessary building block of proteins, and proteins are necessary for building the bodies of plants and animals. But neither plants nor animals can absorb nitrogen from the air! How do they get it, then, so they can have protein? Tiny bacteria in the SOIL absorb the air that is trapped in tiny pockets in the soil. These bacteria are called "nitrogen fixers." The nitrogen fixers take the nitrogen from the air trapped in the soil and change it into a type of nitrogen that can be absorbed through the roots of plants. Animals then can only get the special type of nitrogen by eating the plants!

When plants and animals die, they become food for another kind of bacteria. These bacteria break down the bodies of dead plants and animals and return their parts to the soil -- including that special type of nitrogen. We call these bacteria the SOIL-MAKERS because they turn the bodies of dead plants and animals back into _____. Then the roots of living plants can absorb the nitrogen again, and living animals can eat the plants and get nitrogen. In this manner, the nitrogen can be used again and again. The _____ - _____ are important parts of the nitrogen CYCLE because without them the nitrogen could not be used over and over again by other plants and animals.

Pull up the soil core tube here. Examine its contents. Draw a profile of its con-

tents in the space below.

Soil is partially made from tiny pieces of rock and dead plants and animals that are being turned into soil by the _____ - _____. (Remember: it is also made up of millions and millions of unseen LIVING bacteria!) The amount and type of SOIL is part of the conditions for life in an area. The plants must be adapted to that type of soil. What are the main parts of this marsh soil? With all this decaying plant material, you would think there would be plenty of that special type of nitrogen available for other plants.

Taste the soil and water here. Does it taste bitter?

Put a piece of the litmus paper in the water. What happens?

The acid here released by the decaying plants prevents the growth of the special bacteria that change nitrogen into a usable type. How do these plants get that special type of nitrogen, then, that they can use for body-building protein? Remember: animals as well as plants release those stored-up types of nitrogen when they decay.

Examine the plants in this area. Can you find any that use the bodies of animals for getting that special type of nitrogen they need for protein? Hint: examine closely those that sparkle in the sunlight and those which have leaves shaped like "pitchers."

STATION NINE. This stump was probably cut when loggers were in this area about 80 years ago, and burned after the lumberjacks left. (Fire is one way in which stored _____ energy from the sun is released as heat.) Now, the SOIL-MAKERS (or decomposers) are working on the stump, breaking it down into the four needs of life. The _____ - _____ live on the light energy from the sun that the tree changed into food and stored while it was alive. So even in death, the tree continues to support life. The soil-makers (or decomposers), such as bacteria, fungus, and insects, break the wood down into air, water, and soil particles -- and release the stored types of carbon (carbo-hydrates) and nitrogen. Then, green plants can begin growing in the tiny pockets of new soil. Their roots also help crumble the wood. The plants use the old stump and the fallen trunk now underground behind it as a part of their source for the basic NEEDS of life.

Can you see what we call a "nurse log" behind and below this stump? Why do you suppose it is called that?

The log is a "nurse log" because it helps supply the basic _____ of life for the new living plants on top of it. As these young plants grow, they will store _____ energy from the sun, some minerals from the _____, CARBON and NITROGEN from the air, and _____ -- the four needs of life. All plants are important parts of the carbon and nitrogen cycles. When they die and begin decaying, their stored needs, like those of the nurse log, will be re-cycled by the soil-makers.

Because this happens over and over again, we talk about the carbon and nitrogen CYCLES. The CARBON and NITROGEN cycles affect the amount and type of soil. The amount and type of soil are parts of the conditions for life in an area. Decomposers are very important in the overall CYCLES of needs-life-death-decay-needs. In particular, you have seen that decomposers act to release two important parts of the air, which were stored up in the bodies of the living plants and animals. The _____ and _____, released again by the decomposers, can be re-used by other living plants and animals.

Many man-made materials -- synthetics -- don't fit into the soil cycle because there are no natural decomposers that can turn the synthetics back into the four needs of life. Synthetics break the soil cycle because the needs of life used to make them cannot be returned to living things.

Make a handful of soil, using any of the following materials, but not using anything from the stump:

leaves	moss
water	lichens
sand	rotting wood
dead plants and animals	

Compare your handful of soil with the soil on the ground here.   Are you a good soil maker?

STATION TEN. Before we go on, let's sum up what we have seen so far. First, there are four NEEDS of life: —————, —————, —————, and —————. The needs of life work in ————————— (things that happen over and over again). And the AMOUNT and TYPE of each of the needs of life in these cycles help make up the CONDITIONS for life in any area.

The ridge you are standing on now was once right along the lakeshore. It was formed by the wind pushing ice and soil this far in during the spring. Another ridge, out along the lakeshore, formed the other rim of a "bathtub" that held water in and kept out most of the waves from the lake.

Kneel and look at the surface of the land between here and the lake. Can you see the ridges? Can you see the other rim of the old bathtub? How many ridges do you see? ————————.

The area in between these ridges was once a marsh. As the marsh plants which were growing here died and were turned into SOIL by the decomposers, the bathtub slowly filled in. As the conditions for life changed (from marsh conditions to drier conditions), different kinds of plants began growing here because they fit the new CONDITIONS for life. Trees started growing here when the "bathtub" started filling in, but the force of the WIND (moving air) can push over even large trees. The trees are not turning this area into a forest yet because they are often pushed over by the ————————.

How much "push" does the wind have? Record the direction and speed of the wind. From the ———— at ———— m.p.h.

Count the number of fallen trees between here and the next stop. Which way did most of them fall?

STATION ELEVEN. Rain and melting snow collect in the lake. The air moving across the surfaces of the ground and the lake picks up some of this water through the evaporation part of the water _____.

> Put your hand in the water and wave it in the air for a speeded-up version of EVAPORATION. When your hand is dry, it also feels cooler than it did before -- it has a lower temperature.

One of the effects of evaporation is a decrease in TEMPERATURE. The temperature of the lake is almost always lower than that of the soil because of evaporation from its surface.

The water in some parts of the lake may be warmer than in other parts. There are cold springs in parts of the lake -- the water near the cold springs has a lower _____. The ice ridge, pushed up by the wind on the unprotected side of the lake, keeps the cold lake water from flowing into the marsh. You could expect the water to be warmer in the marsh than in the lake -- its temperature would be higher. The water in the marsh is also shallower, so the _____ energy from the sun can warm it faster. It takes longer for the light energy from the sun to warm the deeper lake water. In short, one of the important CONDITIONS for life found in the marsh is warm water.

> Look for the break in the outer rim of the "bathtub." What plants can you see that tell you the water is deeper beyond the ridge? Measure and record the depth of the water in the marsh: _____ inches. What is its temperature at the bottom? _____° At the surface? _____°.

STATION TWELVE. All energy flows from the sun. Energy is what makes things change (grow, move, or become warmer). You have seen how the sun produces LIGHT energy, and LIGHT energy gives off heat. Without _____ energy there would be no food. The plants need light energy to split the water parts inside their leaves into hydrogen and oxygen. The plants need light energy to combine the hydrogen with the carbon dioxide from the air to form a carbo-hydrate. The plants need light energy to release oxygen and absorb carbon dioxide.

The leaves on some of the plants here have been partly covered up. Carefully examine what happens when the leaf of a green plant can't get light energy from the sun. Can the leaf make food without light?

Animals need the food and oxygen produced by the plants with light energy. Animals also need light energy for heat and for vision.

Without light energy, there would be no HEAT. It is the HEAT from light energy that melts the frozen water and thaws the frozen ground. When plants and animals decay, the soil-makers break down their bodies and give off HEAT. Any time something made by light energy is broken down, its stored light energy is released as _____.
When fuel is burned, the energy released is really stored light energy, but there is only a certain amount of light energy stored in wood, coal, and oil. Man uses this up faster than it can be replaced.

Man has tampered with the energy flow in another way, too. Earth's nightly heat loss keeps the temperature of the earth about the same all of the time -- if none of the heat escaped, the earth would get hotter every day until nothing could live. Just the right amount of heat is held in by a "blanket" of air. But many scientists are worried that, as the blanket of air becomes polluted, it won't be able to work the same way. (When man pollutes, he introduces things into the cycle that weren't there naturally.) The polluted air may either hold in too much heat, making the earth much warmer, or not let in enough of the light energy from the sun -- making the earth much colder. This is just one example of how man's actions can break the cycle of life by introducing things into a cycle that aren't there naturally. This is called pollution, and pollution can create conditions that may destroy life.

As you go down this ridge, notice the flattened, "upended" roots area in the small inlet. What is happening here?

STATION THIRTEEN. The green and white things growing on this tree are called "lichen." Lichen is partly a plant called algae, which is green because it contains green FOOD-MAKING parts -- and partly a fungus, which is white because it has no green _____ - _____ parts. The green algae part of the lichen can make food, using the sun's light energy plus air; but it could not grow on the tree without the help (or COOPERATION) of the fungus. Where does the green algae part of the lichen get the other two basic needs -- the soil and water? The FUNGUS helps soak up the water that falls as rain and helps break down a tiny bit of the tree bark in order to get minerals for the food-making parts of the green ALGAE. So the green algae and the white fungus work together in order to survive.

The lichen is a special example of cooperation because the algae and the fungus are really parts of the same living thing. Often, separate living things -- even a plant and an animal -- work together to help each other meet the CONDITIONS for life. The algae and the fungus have ADAPTED to the _____ for life on the tree by taking a special FORM. The many FORMS of life are the ways in which different things adapt to the different sets of conditions for life.

Gently peel back a piece of the lichen from the tree. Is it taking any food or water from the tree? Do you see how important cooperation is to the lichen? What would happen if the green part could not make food or the white part could not collect water?

Chew a piece of lichen. How does it taste? Can you figure out why?

STATION FOURTEEN. Soil is made from tiny pieces of ROCK mixed with the remains of dead plants and animals. Pieces of rock are broken off by the forces of wind, water, and ice. We say that the forces of _____, _____, and _____ are important soil-making helpers, because they break down rock. Soil-makers (decomposers) break down dead plants and animals into the basic needs of life--soil, water, and air, plus stored light energy (heat). The thickness of the layer of soil, the amount of sand or rock pieces in it, and the amount of decaying plants and animals help to make up the CONDITIONS for life. Plants must be adapted to sandy soil to be able to grow in places where the conditions for life include soil that is mostly sand. Plants must be adapted to small amounts of certain minerals if there is a small amount of those minerals in the soil. The AMOUNT and TYPE of soil is part of the conditions for life in an area. The plants must be adapted to the _____ and _____ of soil in an area in order to live there.

Pull up the soil core tube here. Go back to the sheet for STATION EIGHT and draw a profile of this soil in the second space. Then compare the soil profiles. How are they different? How are they alike?

Put a small amount of the soil from the tube into the larger "well" of the soil testing kit; add a drop of the chemical and wait, then tilt the kit so the liquid runs into the smaller well. What happens? Compare this soil with the soil you found in the marsh.

The differences between the soil of the marsh and the soil of the forest partly explain the differences in the FORMS of life that grow in the two places. So the many varieties of soil are part of the reason for the wide differences in the FORMS of life in the world.

Look here for the only tree of its kind in this section of the forest. (It's wearing a red collar!) Why is there only one small tree of this kind here, while at Woodland there are many of the same kind that grow over 80 feet high?

STATION FIFTEEN. The AMOUNT of heat in the air is part of the CONDITIONS for life here -- the temperature of the air is an indicator of the amount of heat in the air. The air is also moving -- the wind blows from a certain direction and has a certain speed. We could say that the TYPE of air is often "moving air" or wind. The AMOUNT and TYPE of air affects the conditions for life here. Both the air temperature and wind are parts of these _____ for life.

Another part of these conditions for life is the water cycle. The AMOUNT of rain that falls here during the summer is important to the plants that live here -- they are adapted to that _____ of rainfall. The amount that falls during each rainfall affects the green plants because they need water to make food, but just like animals they can drown if there is too much water.

How much rain fell here the last time it rained? Record the amount of the last

rainfall: _____ inches. If all the rain for the summer fell at once, what would it

look like here?

The plants have grown to fit these conditions for life; they are adapted to having several rainfalls about like the one you measured in the rain gauge. Other plants have to be adapted to the conditions for life in an area where all the rain falls at once. The TYPE of water is as important as the AMOUNT of water.

Water pollution occurs when man puts anything into the water cycle that isn't there naturally. If the water is polluted, many plants and animals cannot live in an area -- they aren't adapted to pollution! Air pollution can also affect the water cycle; pollution can cause more of the water in the clouds to fall as precipitation. When man pollutes the air, he may also affect the water cycle by changing the amount of water that falls in an area. Again, the natural cycle is broken. Whenever man breaks the cycle of life by putting in things that aren't there naturally, he changes the CONDITIONS for life. Sometimes the conditions he creates will no longer support life at all.

Both the _____ and _____ of each NEED of life make up the CON-DITIONS for life in an area. The _____ for life then help determine the FORMS of life that develop there.

STATION SIXTEEN. Without LIGHT energy from the sun, plants cannot make food. Without _____ energy, their food-making parts cannot change air, water, and soil into food. Since only a certain amount of light from the sun falls on an area, the plants compete for the light energy, sometimes crowding each other out. In shady areas, certain large plants (like some kinds of trees) are blocking out most of the sun from the ground, and only shade-loving plants can grow. The trees make a kind of roof blocking out much, but not all, of the sun's LIGHT energy. Some plants can live in these shady areas because they have grown to fit or ADAPTED to places where there is less light energy. Often, they have broader leaves to catch every ray of sunlight that comes through the "roof" (or canopy). They have grown to fit to living where there is less sunlight by having certain FORMS. The amount of sunlight affects the conditions of life in an area because different plants are _____ to different amounts of sunlight. Plants growing in sunny areas may have smaller leaves, because for them, getting enough light energy is no problem. They couldn't live in a less sunny place because they are not adapted to the shade. They are adapted to sunny places. So when trees start growing where there are mostly plants adapted to plenty of sun, soon these plants can't get enough light energy to produce food -- the trees' canopy blocks it off. Plants that need a lot of sun stop growing there and plants that are adapted to the new conditions for life take over. As the conditions for life change, the FORMS of life will change: _____ of life which are better adapted to the new conditions will replace the forms of life that were adapted to the old conditions.

Look at the area on your right. Does it look the same as the forest you were walking through at first? Are the forms of life there the same as those living in the marsh to your left? Now, look through the canopy. Which canopy has the most holes?   Why?

STATION SEVENTEEN. This ridge was formed by wind pushing up the ice on the lake in the spring long ago. The sand in the ridge is one sign that this part of the forest was once the edge of the lake; before that, perhaps, the ridge separated a marsh from the lake. Decaying plants, being turned into _____ by the soil-makers slowly filled in the marsh. As the soil was formed and the marsh slowly filled in, other kinds of plants began replacing the marsh plants. The marsh plants, growing and decaying, actually changed the CONDITIONS for life until the land was so dry that the marsh plants were no longer adapted to the new _____ for life which they had helped CHANGE. (This is one example of how plants themselves _____ the conditions for life.) Then, as the conditions for life changed, plants that were ADAPTED to the drier soil competed with the marsh plants. Since they were better _____ to the conditions for life in the forest, they "won" in competing for the basic needs of life. Competing and adapting are important parts of plant SUCCESSION. When one form of plant life is replaced by another that is better adapted to changing conditions brought on by the maturity of those plants, what happens is called plant SUCCESSION. Plant succession will continue as new plants replace the ones growing here now. When the CONDITIONS for life in an area change, the FORMS of life CHANGE because plants that are adapted to the new conditions compete with old plants. The FORMS of life _____ when the _____ for life change. A change in conditions for life will usually cause a change in the _____ of life in an area.

Did you notice a change in the amount of sunlight as you walked up the ridge? One thing that changes as a marsh fills in and becomes a forest is the amount of light energy that reaches the ground. In the forest, the trees' canopy blocks out more of the light energy.

Can you find any evidence in the exposed part of this ridge that would show that this area was once a beach?

Are the pebbles smooth or rough?

Would the stones along a beach be smooth or rough?

STATION EIGHTEEN.

Climb the observation tower and look out over the marsh. Watch the air moving over the long grasses. Looking out from the tower, what evidence can you find that tells you something about the moving air?

Can you spot three pieces of evidence?

This is a marsh partly because of the moving air. The wind pushed up a ridge to separate the marsh from the lake. Can you see the high point of the ridge on the far side of the marsh? The marsh has a special set of _____ for life. The plants out in the marsh must be _____ to those conditions for life. Look over to the opposite shore of the lake. Why are trees growing there -- why isn't that a marsh? The wind blows mostly from across the lake because in this part of the world the wind is usually blowing from the west. The shoreline across the lake is sheltered from the _____ by the trees. In the spring, when the wind pushes the ice into shore, the area across the lake is sheltered from the wind so no ice ridges are formed to separate a marsh from the lake.

The marsh plants are slowly filling in this marsh. As the plants die and are turned into _____ by the decomposers, the marsh will CHANGE. Then, other plants which are adapted to the changing conditions for life will begin to grow. CHANGE in the conditions for life is an important part of plant SUCCESSION. When the conditions for life _____, different FORMS of life will move in. This is called plant _____, because new plants will replace the ones growing here now. Plant succession, then, means that different _____ of plant life begin growing as the conditions for life change. And as the different forms of plant life begin growing, different animals will start living here to feed on the new plants. So changes in the conditions for life cause changes in the forms of life, both animal life and plant life.

123

STATION NINETEEN. Without LIGHT, you could not be reading this; without LIGHT energy from the sun, you could not be standing here at all! The SUN is the source of energy for all life. All energy flows from the _____. The green food-making parts of the plants use light energy from the sun to make FOOD from water, soil, and carbon dioxide. The plants store some of this food and use some of it to grow. When you eat food, you are really eating stored _____ energy from the sun. Your body breaks the FOOD back down into water, soil, and carbon dioxide, releasing the energy which you need to live. So the energy which you need to live comes from the sun, too.

Animals cannot live with only light, air, water and soil, because they cannot use the light energy from the sun to change the air, water and soil into food. Only green plants can use _____ energy to make food. Without tools, animals can only use the sun's energy to see and to be warm (and maybe get a suntan!) Animals must eat green _____ or eat animals that eat green _____ or eat the animals that eat the animals that eat green plants! Animals depend on green plants for the energy they need. Animals also depend on green plants for another one of their needs -- the type of AIR that they need.

Remember that plants use the carbon dioxide part of the air and give off the part of the air called oxygen. Animals use the oxygen to live and give off carbon dioxide. So animals and plants cooperate with each other in getting the different types of air that they each need.

Can you use the soil to make food? A green plant can, with light, carbon dioxide, and water. Can you use the light energy from the sun to make food? The plant can, because it has green food-making parts that can make food from light, water, soil, and the _____ from the air. Both you and the plant can use water to live. And you depend on each other for the part of the air that each needs. You breathe in oxygen and breathe out carbon dioxide. The plant breathes in _____ _____ , which is just the opposite of what you do. What would happen if there were no green plants? What would happen if there were no animals?

Remember the "box of life" that you opened at the beginning of the trail? Make your own box of life now, and include the one thing that ANIMALS need besides the four basic needs of all life. (Animals depend on plants for food, so be sure to include one in your special "box of life" for animals.) Cup your hands and use them as the box.

STATION TWENTY. All life has the same basic needs -- light, air, water and soil. We call these the NEEDS of life. The AMOUNT and TYPE of each of these needs of life determine the conditions for life in an area. The _____ and ____ _____ of water in an area, for example, affects the conditions for life there. The amount and type of the other needs of life -- light, air, and soil -- also help make up the CONDITIONS for life. The needs of life work in CYCLES -- things that happen over and over again. We say that evaporation, condensation, and precipitation make up the water _____ because they happen over and over again. Green plants making food and animals digesting food are part of the energy _____ -- because all energy flows from the sun, but the light from the sun is changed to food by the green plants. It can then be used by animals, and this, too, happens over and over again. Then decomposing is important because the basic needs stored in dead plants and animals can be returned to the soil to be used by living things again; decomposition is part of the soil _____. Green plants giving off oxygen which animals need and animals giving off carbon dioxide which green plants need are part of the _____ of air.

Sometimes man breaks the cycles by putting in things that aren't there naturally. When this happens, we say that man pollutes his environment.

Everything grows to fit the place it lives -- it is ADAPTED to living there. A plant cannot grow in a place unless it is _____ to living there. A plant cannot grow in a place unless it is adapted to that place -- it must fit the conditions for life in order to live there. When the CONDITIONS for life change, the old plants may be replaced by other FORMS of plant life which are better _____ to the changing _____ for life. When the conditions for life change, then, the _____ of life change to meet those conditions.

Walk on up to the plotting board. Record the data you have gathered on the ENVIRONMENTAL STUDY TRAIL PLOTTING BOARD. Compare your data with that gathered earlier.

You have seen that there are four basic NEEDS of life, that the needs of life work in CYCLES, that the cycles set the CONDITIONS for life, and how the FORMS of life CHANGE in order to meet those conditions for life.

As you walk back along the trail, take your time and notice some of the other features of the lake, forest, and marsh communities. What you have seen about needs, cycles, conditions, change, and forms of life may help you see everything that lives here more clearly. Each plant and each animal is a part of the community. Each has needs; each has a place where it is; and each must change to fit changing conditions in order to survive.

As you walk, you may also want to think about your own place in the cycle of life -- your needs -- how you adapt to certain conditions -- how you change. As you breathe, think about the cycle of air between you and the plants. Feel the sun and the wind and the water. Feel the trail change underfoot as you move from one kind of soil to another. Be aware of the life that is all around, and of the invisible forces that you have "seen" behind the outward appearances of this area.

(Remember to return the paper towels at stop 3 to their container after checking on the process of evaporation! When you get back, return your clipboards to the A-frame.)

The Environmental Study Trail was designed as a self-guiding trail for those who want a combination of sensory and conceptual learning that uses data-gathering equipment. We chose a programmed learning format, an unusual development for trail systems, but by writing in an appropriate response occasionally the participant goes beyond passive reading to an active, involved role with the written material. The interpretive and data-gathering activities included in the trail can stand alone, but the explanatory material adds greatly to the depth of the trail. It heightens the campers' understanding of the "inner workings" of the ecosystem. And because it is written with the concept *building* approach, starting with simple frames and gradually adding more data, it helps make the ideas easier to grasp. Meanwhile, references to specific features of the landscape, and the information gathered directly by the participant, remove such key words as "cycles," "adaptation," and "conditions" from the realm of the abstract and place them securely in the immediate surroundings -- which is exactly where they operate.

Walking the trail, participating in the programmed learning, looking for details of the landscape, performing experiments and interpreting the results -- this is an experience in total learning. Concepts are introduced, assimilated, and applied, all in one afternoon!

general   •the route for this Environmental Study Trail goes along a lakeshore; a boardwalk leads into the marsh. The trail passes through a varied forest community and follows the line of an old "ice ridge" for part of its distance. With modifications, the trail material and approach can be used in any area.

•the readings are designed to build concepts sequentially, so their basic order should be retained.

•the interpretive material is geared to the features of this particular trail; examples of land formation, communities, adaptation, etc., should be geared to the specific area -- and every area has details worth noting! See Watts, *Reading the Landscape*, for ideas.

•in most cases, the data-gathering is keyed into and supports the programmed-learning material.

•to conserve paper, laminate several sets of your station sheets, and have the participants use grease pencils.

laying out
the trail   •prepare 20 index cards, numbered for the stops on the trail. On the appropriate cards, list the specific data-gathering materials needed and the type of interpretive details desired (land formation, wind, decomposition, etc.), and also note possible substitutions: a lichen-covered rock could be substituted for the lichen-covered tree at station thirteen, for example.

•Now, walk along the trail, noting possible locations for each station. Try to keep them evenly spaced -- but yield to the requirements of the landscape! If some stops don't seem to fit at all, re-think possible substitutions (some are listed in the following guidelines).

•the EST is about 3/4 mile long, 3 feet wide. Posts for the twenty numbered stops are of pine, 4-5 inches thick, 5-6 feet long, tops cut off at an angle with the number routed in, then painted yellow.

•boardwalks are built across areas of the marsh, primarily to keep traffic damage to the community at a minimum. The boardwalks are low, almost at water level. They are built by placing and staking 30" logs about seven feet apart along the desired route, then laying 8' planks across them and nailing them in. The planks are 2" thick; two planks, each a foot wide, make up one section of the boardwalk. Use rough-cut pine and a preserving agent on parts that would be in contact with water.

station one   a large windfall was named the "magic mountain" because of the lush growth of moss, lichen, and small plants that it supports. Almost any nurse log or stump could fill the bill. (Or simply stake out another example of a micro-community: ten square feet of earth, perhaps, and change the introduction accordingly.)

station two   ●"the needs of life" box is 1' square, with the two messages painted on its hinged cover.

station three   ●cut paper towels in narrow strips, so several can be hung up at once. A small plastic "bin" keeps them damp while stored.

●a rain gauge which records total precipitation (cumulative) is also mounted on a post at this stop.

station four   ●place one rain gauge in the forest; another in a clearing, for comparison.

●use old stumps. Cut fresh surfaces with a bucksaw, for easier counting.

station five   ●attach a rear-view mirror from an old car to a post.

station six   ●place a wind vane in a relatively open area.

●place the two pinwheels, one in the open and one back in the forest; if necessary, indicate the location of the latter.

station seven   ●a regular outdoor thermometer is attached to the post. An aquarium thermometer floats on the surface of the water, attached to a line that can be pulled in. The soil thermometer is kept in the ground, its location indicated by a sign.

●this station was designed for use on the boardwalk; adapt it to a dry area by substituting various surfaces to be compared: sand, dirt, grass, moss, sun, shade.

station eight •a soil core tube is kept in the soil at the edge of the marsh. This stop, too, could be changed to emphasize a different set of special conditions for life and the adaptations which have been made to meet those conditions.

•litmus paper is kept in a small waterproof vial attached to the post; supply is re-stocked regularly.

station nine •the trail includes an old stump, behind which a small hump reveals the presence of the "nurse log" (known by some as a "cradle knoll"). The opening line about lumberjacks can be altered to suit the situation. If there is no nurse log, the three sentences (beginning with "Can you see . .") can be omitted without breaking the flow.

station ten •this wind vane is in an area that is more open than the forest, yet not so open as the marsh. Most of the trees have fallen during heavy storms.

station eleven •a measuring stick has one thermometer attached to its base, while another thermometer is attached to the post itself.

station twelve • a "sun-screen" deprives some of the leaves of light.

station fourteen •another soil core tube is kept here; the soil testing kit is the type often sold for home gardeners.

station fifteen • the "last" rainfall; obviously, this should be emptied.

station eighteen • the observation tower stands about eight feet above ground level, just high enough for a good view.

CRUSOE CAMP

I could hear the suction of whirlpools created by my paddle. It was that silent.

Around the campfire one night, Harry explained about the Pueblo Indians and the one lady he met. The lady said that the earth was a part of her, but she could not explain why or how she knew. Well, now I know why she knew that she was a part of the earth and how, too, because now -- I am also a part of the earth.

I think that when you were out there you became totally aware of everything that went on around you. You heard sounds you didn't hear before and saw things you didn't see before. We spent a lot of time alone -- out there, alone, you can do a lot of things you couldn't do if there were a lot of people around.

I got up on top of a stump and flapped my arms like a bird. It was cool.

I'm by myself now. The trees are rustling across the river and there's a bed of moss. It's quiet and I'm like in a world by myself. I feel like Robinson Crusoe.

Crusoe Camp is on an island, but it need not be surrounded by water. It is, above all, an island of wilderness -- a place unreached by those who travel by car. It must be large enough to house six teenagers and an adult and give them room to be alone. It must have trees and sky and places to explore. That's really all that is required of the island.

The people who go to Crusoe Camp -- who are they, and what do they take? There is one adult who is the leader, guide, and friend; there are six young people who are old enough to begin asking important questions about themselves and about life. They take to the island only simple shelters, simple food, and simple tools.

Why do they go? To look for answers to questions, perhaps. They go to live simply and to be in contact with the most basic needs of human existence, the roots of human experience, and to benefit from a temporary isolation from their society. They go in order to live *with* nature, not merely *in* nature. In doing so, they hope to learn about themselves.

Crusoe Camp is a four-day experience in just that: living with nature and learning about nature's ways and one's own. Every activity helps the person who goes there focus on becoming more aware, closer to nature, and closer to himself. In this setting, with these goals in mind, the inputs flow together and build upon each other, to make Crusoe Camp a very lasting part of one's life.

It's an incredibly quiet place, almost eerie at first. It's a very special place without motors or bells or sirens or even loud voices. But one gets used to it. One begins to hear smaller noises, less intrusive sounds, like the trill of a bird or the faint rustling of aspen leaves. In the silence and the soft soothingness of natural voices, one can begin to think and to feel.

Crusoe Camp IS an island.

The quiet paddle into Crusoe Camp put us in the mood of the wilderness. On the way, we saw beaver lodges, osprey, and eagles. It was really great to be back to basics. The whole pace is so relaxed and unhurried . . . everything is so calm. We took our time going there. When we got around the last bend to where Crusoe Camp is, it looked just like I'd hoped it would.

SILENT PADDLE. We canoe silently to our island, just listening and watching.

"Welcome to Crusoe Camp."

"Crusoe Camp -- if you give it a chance -- is a very personal kind of experience. It's like nothing you've ever done before. Basically, it's an experience in living closely with nature. If you just look behind me here, over the open water to the shore, you might begin to sense where we're going. We'll be canoeing down this river to a very special place -- Crusoe Camp.

"When we go, it's like we are going into a new world, leaving behind the old and entering freshly into the new. That new world is the world of nature. Just let go of the old and open your mind to the new. Listen for the natural voices. So often, we hear parents' voices, teachers' voices, TV and radio voices, but on Crusoe we listen for natural voices: the wind in the trees -- the splash of a deer in the creek. Be open to receiving these voices.

"Because we're going into a new world, and so we can hear the natural voices, we paddle into Crusoe Camp silently. For the silent paddle, tie your soft tool (bandana) around the paddle. When you get into the canoe, just slide the soft tool to where you think it needs to be to keep the paddle from whacking against the side. So if the paddle does happen to hit, the soft tool will muffle the sound and remind us of the need to be silent. Our soft tools will help us enter the new world as quietly as we can. And since this is a silent paddle, we won't talk unless it's really needed. When necessary, we can use sign language to communicate with one another without speech. Instead of talking, listen, and hear the voices of nature.

"Also, stay in the here and now. Be here, now. Be content with what's happening in the present and be open to it. The whole tone of Crusoe is like that -- open, aware, relaxed, simple, free. So we begin by paddling silently and being open to all the beauty around us, and every silent stroke of the paddle brings us a little closer to Crusoe Camp. Think about it as we go -- we're entering a new world. Okay? Let's go!"

133

Here, the rules of nature come out much stronger . . . these are the rules that will never change. You just do what nature does, just living by it. I think that's what we're trying to do here. I feel a lot closer to nature.

I feel like this place is mine to live, and now to observe it and love it. I see it natural and wild. As a friend. All of it as a friend. Good-bye, friend. I'll miss you, but I'll remember you, too.

EARTH HOUSEHOLD. Taking care of our island -- watching out for it -- living with it instead of against it.

"Here, we are on an island, and looking around you can see its beauty and its unspoiledness. But it's easy to see how we could destroy it if we aren't careful. If we walked just anywhere, we'd trample all the ferns -- so we stay on the paths. If we made fires everywhere, it would soon be ugly -- so we have one fire, here, and light it only when we need it. If we went to the bathroom everywhere, the island would soon be uninhabitable -- so we dig one latrine and use it. We pack out all litter. We gather our firewood carefully and away from the island. We don't tear up living things or disturb the wildlife or yell and scream a lot. This may all seem strict, but it's basic wilderness manners. It's important also to remember that everything we do affects this island: everything goes somewhere. That's one of Nature's rules. Anything we leave here, or destroy here, changes the balance a little bit. We need to think about what we do.

"When we leave the island, we want it to look as fresh and as clean as when we first came to it. When we get into the canoes to leave, we'll even cover up our footprints on the beach -- we don't want to leave any sign of our having been here.

"With the restraint, there is also a great gain -- one not often had by 20th century humans. We'll know we're trying to live within the balance of nature, so we'll feel more a part of it. And, in a small way, we'll feel that we really belong here, because we are sensitive enough to have a place that we keep clean, keep it the way it should be.

"To start out, let's hide our canoes. This will make our presence here less noticeable, and it will also help us think about this island as our home by breaking off one of our ties with civilization. This island is where we will live -- it is our home. The word 'ecology' comes from the Greek word for a house. Ecology is, then, a kind of science of good housekeeping.

"Earth household."

Hammock's finished, and I am in it for the first time. Fantastic! Really great, the feeling it gives you. There is no noise to detect any type of human life. Here I am, suspended four feet off the ground, surrounded by nature and her songs. Any jerk is just engulfed by the hammock and changed into a smooth flowing motion, like a stone landing in a lake.

SHELTER. A home, a dwelling, a place of our own.

"Our shelters are hammocks. It is important to learn to be alone and to be able to be comfortable alone. Solitude is something we rarely get a chance to experience anymore. Here, on Crusoe Camp, we each have a spot on the island as 'our place,' where we can listen to the frogs and birds and wind by ourselves at night.

"Shelter is basic and necessary and important. Our shelters are simple -- we don't need much. Can you have a more elegant home than trees and sky? In being alone in hammocks, we learn about ourselves. By living simply, shucking off the paraphernalia, we see and feel the basic patterns of seeking shelter from rain, of getting ready for bed, of sleeping and rising. By being alone, we are more aware of these parts of our lives. We feel them all."

Had a great walk. Sat down, closed eyes, and just listened to different sounds. Tuning some in and some out, constantly changing and holding on to sounds. Then I made friends with a piece of driftwood and later with a rock. After the walk, I came over and sat on this stump and started writing. It is really cool right now because the sun is shining off the dew drops hanging on the grass.

You look in between the branches and you see the spaces. Then you're sort of more aware of the shape, the whole tree, things you wouldn't notice normally.

SENSING WALK. A vehicle for heightening sensory awareness.

"On a sensing walk, we are silent. We'll walk along at a slow pace, just taking things in, opening our senses. Then, at different points along the way, we'll stop for some special inputs that may help us be more aware of our senses and what they can tell us about this place.

"First, let's sit and relax here for a while. Focus on a tree that you can see from where you're sitting. Examine its trunk and branches. Just look at it. Take it all in, slowly . . . Now, instead of seeing the tree, try to see the SPACES around the tree. Look at the sky between the leaves or branches. Look behind and above the tree. Again, go slowly . . . You'll know you're on target when the tree suddenly seems to leap forward. Sometimes it takes a while . . . This is something you can try again when you're out on your own.

"Now, let's lie down in a relaxed way. Close your eyes and listen. Focus on different sounds, one at a time. Try not to label them, but just experience their clarity and richness. Then with your mind, weave these sounds in and out. Let them blend together. Now, focus on different ones; turn the volume up and down by your awareness and concentration. You can create your own symphony of sounds.

"Let's pause here. Everyone find a natural object. Slowly, feel it . . . hold it in your hand . . . turn it over . . . smell it . . . taste it . . . handle it . . . put it on your forehead . . . rub it against your cheek . . . hold it up to the sky . . . put it in your mouth . . . hold it against your ears . . . feel its weight on your face, your chest, your eyelids . . . sense its color and texture. Get to know it in as many ways as possible. It's like you've just made a new friend."

They're practically all you need. You don't need anything else, really. You can do anything with the knife, and the soft tool is handy, too, because you can wash your hands and dry them off, or pick up hot pans. They just come in handy sometimes. It's sort of neat to be left with tools like Robinson Crusoe was. Just simple tools -- and getting along with them.

TOOLS. Objects made by man to help him live.

"Man is called HOMO SAPIENS -- the wise one, the one who thinks. But perhaps he should be called HOMO FABER, the tool-maker, or the one who makes tools.

"We use tools every day. They are vital to our survival. Think of the different tools we've used today -- canoes, paddles, hammocks, our soft tool (bandana) for softening sounds, cooking utensils -- and the tools that were used to make the other tools we use! All are tools. At Crusoe Camp we focus on a few simple tools: your soft tool, for washing and cleaning; your journal, the tool for self-expression; and your jackknife, for carving and making things.

"We each have a soft tool now. You can use it for whatever you want. If the bugs are bothering you, you can wear it around your neck. Or you can dip it in the water and put it over your head to keep cool. You can dry your hands with it. In short, you can use it in as many ways as you want. These are yours to keep for the trip, so take care of them. I wear mine hanging from my back pocket. It works pretty well, 'cause then if you need it, you can just whip it out. Soft tool. Okay?

"This is what you can call your hard tool. You already have your soft tool, and this is your hard tool. It's a jackknife, and you have to be very careful when you use it. You'll each get one, along with a sharpening stone and a small draw-string bag. When you're carving, always carve away from you. That way, if you miss and slip, you're not going to hurt yourself. We care for our hard tools at Crusoe Camp. That means we don't play with them or throw them around or lose them, and we keep them sharp because we use them almost every day. To sharpen the jackknife, moisten the whetstone and rub the knife against it in a circular motion, away from you, and almost flat against the stone. Keep the whetstone and your jackknife in the cloth bag; you can wear it very easily through a belt loop and you won't lose it.

"We talk about the hard tool and the soft tool because they are simple tools that you can use often. They can also remind you of other tools you use, and how you use them. Tools can help us live and create, or they can be destructive or unsafe. Think about tools."

I want to write out here. Sometimes, like at school, they make you write. I usually don't like writing in general, but writing a trip log, and going on trips like this, I want to write about the high points. It helps me remember. I want to write in it, and it keeps me company and I'm writing all my thoughts down, and it's fun. You can do something much easier if you want to do it.

JOURNAL. The record in the young person's own words of his experiences.

"Robinson Crusoe kept a journal about the way he lived on his island, what he did, and the thoughts that were going through his mind. We keep journals, too. Your journal is another TOOL you have at Crusoe Camp, a tool for expressing yourself. It is your friend, too -- to talk to when you're alone. It's also your own record of your experiences here. Don't worry about grammar or spelling. The journal is a tool for you -- to express youself in your own words. Use it in the way that feels best to you.

"There will be time every night after dinner for writing, when you can sit back and kind of think things over. Take your journal with you when you go out, too, so that it's always with you when you feel like putting something in it. You can write haiku or draw pictures or ask questions or write your feelings about all that is happening."

Anyone can be really complicated, Anyone can get away from the basics. It takes a lot of doing to get down to the really basic things and really think about them. With our ancestors, it was easy for them to get down to the basics, but we're getting farther away and it's getting harder. Now it's just as hard to get up, away from the basics. Hard. Now we're stuck up there and it's hard to get down again. It's like a staircase that each step is disappearing as you go up.

There's a lot to be learned.

CRUSOE CAMPFIRE. The first night -- an introduction to Crusoe Camp.

"Perhaps you have read or heard the story of Robinson Crusoe. He lived alone on an island for 24 years. He made most of his own tools and raised or gathered his own food. He lived alone and peacefully with the natural world for a long time.

"This is the basis for our Crusoe Camp. We are here to learn about nature, be close to her, and feel her moods and ways. We live harmoniously, easily, and simply here in an open, relaxed way. It is an experience of being at home, at one, and at peace as a fellow species in the natural world.

"We don't push or shove or compete. Crusoe Camp is a natural way to open up and grow, to learn about our senses and our bodies and about the world around us.

"We're going to have some really neat and unusual experiences while we live at Crusoe Camp -- just as Robinson Crusoe did on his island. I would like to read to you this evening about one of his experiences . . ."

I got out in some of those great big grasses out there, and I got down on my hands and knees and crawled through them for a little while. I really didn't know where I was going. When you get down, like an animal, it's hard to know where you're going. So I decided I'd make a map of the area. I went in a circle and I found my way around pretty well. Then I drew the map up on my paper and I drew where the logs were and everything else. I did that all while I was crawling; and then I got up and made a map, and I was surprised how accurate I was.

EXPLORATION. Finding the new, seeking the unknown, and learning about the area.

"The rough map that I've drawn in the sand represents this area: here's the river, the bluff, the general outline of the island -- and here's where we are right now. There are a lot of blank spaces on the map; you'll get a chance to explore some of them this afternoon.

"In exploring, we are getting in touch with an ancient art, discovery. This continent was discovered by men exploring for different reasons, but often just because they loved to seek out the unknown. We, too, seek new places and go to see areas we've never seen before. Exploration, poking around, wandering and looking are perhaps among man's deepest pleasures and deepest needs.

"There's a lot here to explore: the islands, where the creek goes and what it does, the animals that call this place home. There are a lot of things to do while you're exploring. You can jot down descriptions or draw a map in your journal; seek out small places that are neat; find a place that can be your 'vision spot;' locate the homes of animals; look for blueberry patches or other wild foods for when we go out gathering. Use your senses, like we did on our walk; maybe make friends with something you find, or listen to a symphony of sounds. Use your imagination. Explore your surroundings in different ways.

"You'll each go alone to do this: find a vision spot, chart an area or note some landmarks, look for food, and locate the homes of animals. Let's say we won't go outside this area -- stay within hailing distance of camp, so when I blow on my horn, you can return to this map in the sand to share your discoveries. Okay? Let's go see what's out there!"

Next on the agenda was berry picking. We went to a bunch of blueberries and eagle's claw. There were thousands of blueberries!

I wandered like a grazing deer from patch to patch of blueberries. It was a while before I stopped eating and started gathering! Soon a rhythm or pattern developed as I picked blueberries and only the young eagle's claws or bracken fern shoots.

GATHERING. Collecting some of our own food from the natural world.

"At Crusoe Camp we gather some of our own food. By gathering, we become more aware of one of our basic needs -- the need for food. It's a lot different from just taking a can of something off a shelf in a store. Here, we sense our closeness to all living things because all living things need food. And we see that we depend on the earth for our food because, by gathering, we get our food directly from nature; we FEEL the closeness to the earth. We are doing what men on earth have always done, but as civilization progressed, we have developed more complicated ways of getting our food, ways that let us forget where it really comes from. In getting back in touch with the ancient ways, perhaps we can feel and can sense the time and energy of centuries of people getting their food this way; because getting food is the most basic, most elemental, thing that man or any other animal does.

"Today we're going to look for young fern heads and cattail shoots like the ones in this basket. While doing this, feel and imagine being a part of a tribe of primitive people, getting food in close contact with the earth, and sharing with the tribe."

141

We went swimming in the creek and also in the low spots in the grass-like area. We went sliding in the warm mud. After that, we all just jumped in a small pool and started splashing. It was really funny. The water was great! Cool, clean, refreshing. Then we all dove off a large rock in different directions. It looked like a flower blooming.

FROLIC. Spontaneous play -- an expression of JOIE DE VIVRE, of coming out, of enjoyment, of play in the highest and best sense.

"Sometimes I feel so full of energy and so full of life that I just want to run and shout, or leap and prance like a deer, or plunge into the water and splash around. We all get that way, and it's great to cut loose sometimes. It can be a lot of fun. Play is an important part of life, but people often forget about how good it is. They may think they've outgrown it, but they haven't -- they've just bottled it up. The thing is, when you do that, you also lose some of that energy and aliveness.

"So frolic -- play -- is an important part of Crusoe. A lot of the things we do here are kind of heavy; they're fun, but they're also a little intense. I'm just telling you this because I want you to know that there's a time for spontaneous fun, too; time to just enjoy being here and being alive and being young. And being together, because that's one of the best parts of frolic: other people. Maybe when we first get up in the morning and return from our individual sites, or when we get back from exploring or gathering, we might all go splashing or running or sliding in the mud or just whatever hits us.

"The time for play is when you feel like it and when you can do it without disturbing someone else's quietness."

Made friends with a small patch of grass by the creek. I got down on my knees and looked straight into it. Then I looked at it from ground level. Unbelievable. I was part of the grass. The creek looked so huge and it seemed that the current was rushing along at a tremendous speed. Then I waded to the other side of the grass and knelt into the water. I put my head into the grass like I did before. The trees were huge. I knew what it was like to be a crawling creature on the earth. I tasted the grass. I smelled it. I even heard it as it brushed across my face. The sensation that I had was absolutely unbelievable.

RELATIONSHIP. Being involved with something outside yourself.

"Relationship is an opportunity for you to become close to some part of the natural world. You will have to decide how you want to use that opportunity. I'm going to give you some ideas if you're uncertain, but do what YOU want, what feels good.

"You might just pick an animal and hang out with him, spend time with him. Go and watch that osprey for an hour. Watch how she flies, hovers, cares for her nest, maybe hunts; or see where her mate is and what he's doing. Or you may want to just follow a frog for the morning. Just follow a frog; see all he does and sense his world of weeds and water. Or track a deer. Study the tracks. Hunt for a sighting, look at the droppings, find a bed, get as close to the deer as you can.

"Or you might make a map of this area, like you did when you were exploring. Cover the ground; know it and try to represent it.

"Or carve something. Spend your time with a piece of wood and your jackknife creating whatever you want. Or you may want to fish. Float down the creek; let your mind flow and your pole go and just poke around.

"We'll have several different times to spend on this, so you could get to know the same stump (or bush or rock) as it is from different angles and at different times: when the sun is high, and as it is setting, and in the moonlight, too. Watch the stump change during the time we are here.

"Or role-play an animal. Get down in the weeds and see the world as a grasshopper might. Pretend you're a deer leaping in the woods, or a fish swimming in the water. Try to feel a little of what it's like to be another animal. Use your senses. Listen for natural voices. Everything is alive. Everything has its own sound, its own way. Your relationship is your choice -- your way -- your time. Use it as you like. Get involved."

After breakfast we started on the bread. Mixing the yeast and the rest was lots of fun. It was great kneading the bread. I really got into it. Right now, the bread is rising for the first time. We are about to go down to the beaver den.

Back at camp. The others pushed off for the beaver lodges and we stayed to tend to the bread. After kneading it some more, we all three went down for a swim. After the other guys got back, we read some Haiku and baked the bread.

BREAD-MAKING. We bake our own bread -- each person has his own loaf.

"Bread is the staff of life. Along with hunting and gathering and exploring, one of man's ancient ways was to bake the grain he had grown. Agriculture was an advance in civilization. It meant that people could stay in one place and cultivate food instead of nomadic wanderings in search of game or edible plants. And men and women baked bread from the grain they grew.

"Today, we too bake bread. We will enter the ancient ways for a time and perhaps sense again that elemental contact with the basics of life. By grinding some of the grain with this METATE and MANO, we will be aware that our food comes from the seeds of the earth. By making the bread with our own hands, we will feel the life that is in it. By kneading the bread -- maybe chanting -- we will feel the life-givingness of our action: nourishment for our bodies, joy in creation, pleasure in kneading, security in knowing there is enough, community in sharing the work and the fruits. Bread-making can be an act of love."

Sunlight shimmering
Glittering off the water
An orange hue -- dusk.

. . .

Dew drops glistening
In the sun, will soon be gone
Until another day.

The reason for the haiku on the other page was just because I felt like it.

HAIKU. A short, descriptive nature poem, often with inner meanings and significances.

"Haiku is a form of poetry through which you can express your impressions of the natural world. To help you get the idea, let's write one together about something we can all see right now. Use your journals to jot things down as we go.

"Begin by naming this scene . . . Now, describe it . . . Name the setting . . . Describe the setting . . . Then describe the feelings you have about this scene. Now, go back through what we've said and written and underline the key words and phrases that really describe the ESSENCE of this scene -- what makes it like it is? Just move these around and play with them in your mind until there are only 17 syllables: one line of five, one of seven, and another line of five. That's all there is to it.

"It doesn't have to be complicated. The important thing is for you to get close to something, feel WITH it and use haiku as a way to express that feeling and sensing. If you work with it, I think it will be a very natural way for you to express your experiences.

"Let's go out, now, and find a scene and try writing a haiku about it. Then we'll all come back here to share our scenes with each other."

While I was looking into the river, trying to decide where to go on my vision quest, I looked up. I saw an eagle flying my way. He abruptly turned and headed towards the ridge and vanished behind the tree line. It may mean something. It may not. But that's where I'll head. . .

Went down toward the ridge. Something made me stop. Then ascended bank. Being alert to all my senses. Soaking it all in. I wanted to go one way, but all of a sudden I changed my mind and went across the path -- and there was the eagle feather.

TOTEM. A natural object symbolizing a bond, a protection, an intimacy.

"A totem is a symbol of your relationship with the natural world. Indians had totems -- they were a kind of special protector in times of danger and represented a special relationship with a part of the natural environment.

"At Crusoe Camp, a totem is a natural object which speaks to you with its beauty. You don't really decide on a totem; it's kind of like the totem finds YOU. It speaks to you when you see it, and represents to you what is happening here. A totem is something durable, and something you can wear or carry. It's something you can take with you wherever you go -- even if you move clear across the country -- to remind you of here. It may be a special stick or stone, a feather, or a bone, or a special seed or shell. In the same way that Indians had a totem -- a special relationship -- we, too, search for our totem and our special relationship with the natural world. Your totem is something, one item, that you can take from here to remind you of this closeness.

"This is my totem. It's an eagle's feather that a friend and I found when we first came to this spot last year. It means a lot to me so I take it with me wherever I go -- to Chicago, and out to Oregon, and back here again -- it reminds me of all this.

"Tomorrow, we'll be having a vision quest. If you had been born an Indian, you might have gone on a traditional vision quest to mark your passage from adolescence to manhood. You would go out alone to a mountaintop for three to five days, fasting and praying -- seeking a vision, a sign from the Great Spirit that lives in all things. You might receive a new name, a foreknowledge, or a powerful totem. And when you came back, your childhood would be over. The vision quest marked a definite passage to a new being, with new rights and responsibilities.

"To prepare for our representation of a vision quest tomorrow, we will want to purify ourselves: in the morning, a cleansing ritual so we are fresh, and then at noon we will have only our own baked bread and water, a small way of fasting which helps us become more aware of our bodies.

"Before we leave for our shelters tonight, I'd like to tell the story of an Indian boy and his vision quest . . ."

I feel a strange newness coming over me. I know that when I leave here to go back, I won't be the same as when I came out here. It's just so peaceful.

I'm not sure why I came here, or why I was led here, but it seems like paradise to me. The view, the ground cover, the wind, the trees, everything is perfect. The wind blows in the trees, the birds sing. The bugs buzz. Around me everything is in harmony. Yes, I believe I've been here before. As though I was supposed to come here again. It's hard to describe -- a very nice, but funny feeling inside.

My body was rushed with an urge to shout out "I am alive!" That joy stayed with me as I stood up and watched the river. My body seemed full of something. This may sound corny or weird especially because I am on my vision quest, but I feel very strongly in everything I've said about this place. Most of it I can't explain.

> VISION QUEST. An afternoon of silence and solitude in a special place.

"At the end of this small meal of bread and water, you will begin your vision quests. Let the bread and water help you become more aware of your body and your senses. Smell your loaf. Take the first bite, and really chew it; feel the texture and taste the bread until you swallow it. Feel it giving new energy to your body. Now, tear off a piece and pass it to the person on your right. Let's share our last meal together before we go out. Pass a piece to your left. Eat only enough to satisfy your hunger now, and save the rest for our meal tonight.

"Last night, we talked about the vision quest of the American Indian. At Crusoe Camp, our vision quest is modified. Instead of three to five days, you will spend just one afternoon alone. This is your time to think a bit about your own identity, who you are and where you are going. You may receive insights about yourself. You may learn new things; you may come back a different person.

"We have purified our bodies by washing, and we've eaten our simple meal. Now, it is time for you to go to your vision spot, the place you have chosen to stay in for the afternoon. Be open to what's going on around you. It isn't easy to be alone, with nothing to be busy doing; but it's when you're alone and your mind and body are quiet that you can really perceive and also really think and feel. Open yourself up -- let it happen.

"The vision quest is the heart of Crusoe Camp. From the time when the sun is highest until it begins to set, you are with yourself in the natural world -- to seek a vision -- to absorb -- to be and grow in your own way."

I like the night when we all sat around the campfire. It was neat, the atmosphere of it. You know something? It really feels good to me when I can express something I feel and have people listen.
I feel content.
I feel glad and content and happy.
I'm tired and I just feel like I'm in nature.
I feel just kind of happy to be here.
I feel really alert -- just so much more aware of everything.
I feel kind of satisfied.
I feel great, that's all!

MAGIC CIRCLE CAMPFIRE. A special time for sharing feelings.

"Let's all hold hands in a circle around the fire.

"We've talked a little about some of the experiences you have had today, and it sounds like some neat things were happening. I'd like for you to share with each other some of the feelings you have. We call this our magic circle because we're sharing the fire together by holding hands, and now we're going to share our feelings. What we'll do is go around the circle, and each person say the words: 'This evening, I feel . . .;' then share with everyone what you are feeling right now. Okay. I'll start out. . . .

"We've gone around the circle once, and some feelings are coming out. Sometimes, though, we find ourselves THINKING instead of FEELING. Stick with your feelings; don't worry about what they are, because if you're feeling something, it's good to let it out. Let the feeling take over from the thinking for a while. Let's go around the circle a couple more times and really concentrate on these feelings. This evening, I feel. . . .

"Good. Those are some deep feelings I heard coming out just now. Let's break off the hand holds and just talk for a while about some of the feelings different people expressed. How do you all feel about the time you spent alone, in silence and solitude, this afternoon?"

One of the purposes of Crusoe Camp is to give young people a chance to simply *be* -- to live and grow at their own pace -- outside of structured or conditoned roles. This includes time to be alone in solitude and time to explore the world in their own way -- to poke and wander and wonder. Since the setting is the natural world, we encourage sharpening senses and getting in touch with bodies; we emphasize being free to perceive the world, each in his own way, without being told how to experience things and without competing. The vision quest is the central input giving this freedom. It is a personal time -- totally free -- restricted only by basic safety concerns and a few suggestions about how to handle it.

This whole experience is set up around a simple, harmonious way of life that blends elements from the lifestyle of Robinson Crusoe with some from that of the American Indian. We begin by paddling our canoes in silence, borrowing from the Indian an appreciation for moving about among the plants and animals without advertising one's presence.

Our shelters are Crusoe-like in that each person has his own home, alone in nature. The experience is also one the Indian would have known well. Much of a person's perception of his environment is lost when there are other people around; having an individual shelter is one of the opportunities for solitude which Crusoe Camp provides. It is an opportunity to be open to sensory stimuli from nature, and particularly to be alone and quiet in the early morning and at night.

Tools are important at Crusoe Camp. Our culture uses huge, gargantuan tools to build bridges and freeways, bulldoze subdivisions, and take men to space. We focus on a jackknife and a bandana, yet the boys returning from a Crusoe Camp appreciate and have really felt the use of tools. They've been close to them. They've used their hands to fashion things for their own use and they've experienced using tools in different ways: to get food (gathering berries in the bandana or making a shish-kabob stick), to be creative (carving and whittling), and to be comfortable (using a bandana for a washcloth).

The rationale behind all this is simply that it is important to feel the natural channels of human energy (gathering food, making bread, using tools) that we have broken away from so abruptly since the Industrial Revolution. It is not that we choose to live like cavemen, but rather that we wish once again to experience the joy and harmony of some of the primitive ways. Essentially what we're doing is paring away the outer layers of culture to revel in its essence.

In addition, we focus on self-expression -- giving young people a journal and encouraging them to write in it. We work with haiku as a means to both focus and express emotion. Listening to haiku makes one more aware of nature. Writing it brings one in close to a plant or an animal or a setting. Haiku brings the individual into a definite, intimate relationship with a part of the environment, and that's what Crusoe Camp is all about.

Much that happens has a serious tone. The activities are interesting and fun, but they have a purpose - to aid the individual in thinking about his lifestyle and place in the world. Crusoe Camp is meant for adolescents, young people who are at the age of questioning about these things. The times of solitude, the silences, the serious moments, the sharing of feelings -- all of these help the individual delve into the core of his own selfhood.

Adolescents, in their search for an adult role, however, often forget about the importance of being young. They neglect frolic, as do so many adults. It has been said that man is only fully man when he is playing. At Crusoe Camp, we take time for play, because we believe in the importance of spontaneous, creative energy. Play, after all, is re-creation -- beginning again and being born again to the sensory experience of the world. Frolic doesn't counteract the more solemn times; they complement each other. And so we go to Crusoe Camp, to return to the old, simple ways for a while, to live in nature, to explore, to feel, and to wonder. To grow.

general

- have a list of what goes on the trip -- nothing else. Do not compromise on your packing list.

- be careful about what is used for a focal point in each input. Unless it is very simple, it will be a distraction rather than a focus.

- most of the inputs are done with the group sitting in a circle. All are done with the group SITTING. There's less tendency to wander, physically and mentally, and less distraction.

- the words written here give the essence of the input. There may be other lines which could be used, other thoughts that could be inserted. But the input should not be much longer than what's here. It's an input, not a mini-lecture.

- whenever an ellipsis (. . .) appears in an input, it indicates a necessary pause. Perhaps a leader's most difficult task is knowing when and how to shut up!

- there are three campfires, each with an input: Crusoe campfire, the first night; Totem campfire, the second night; and Magic Circle campfire the last night. The fires are very small for these -- just large enough for everyone to fit around. Small chunks of wood are at hand to feed the fire, but when sitting that close, you don't want it too hot! Nightly camp-fires are traditional when living outdoors -- but they often degenerate into sessions for telling ghost stories and dirty jokes. At Crusoe Camp, each of the evening campfires helps carry out the very special tone that makes Crusoe Camp what it is -- a rich and meaningful experience.

silent
paddle

- the soft tool is a bandana, a foot-square piece of plain-colored cloth with hemmed edges. The cloth should be light, but sturdy. Distribute them after the input.

- for this input, the circle is formed around a sun-shaped stack of pad-dles. Most of the inputs at Crusoe take place with a circle, always with something to focus on.

- there is only a short distance to canoe to the site, not a long, exhausting haul that consumes time as well as energy. The importance of the trip is what happens once we get there -- not the number of miles we paddled.

- paddle in slowly as well as silently. The lead canoe sets a leisurely pace. We concentrate more on the sights and sounds than on speed.

earth
household

- for this input, the circle is formed with the leader on the edge, facing the lake. The campers can focus on the island . . . each will see it a lit-tle differently, each from his own angle.

- we hide the canoes for two reasons: first, so our presence is unob-trusive -- someone passing by might not even know we are there. Secondly, we don't need them; we'll do all our exploring on foot.

●the size of the fires we build at Crusoe Camp fits in with the idea of earth household. We don't want to use more wood than we need. The fire is always just big enough for the need we have and no larger. The evening campfires are very small; we can all sit around them comfortably in a closed circle.

shelter

●shelters are individual. We use hammocks, but there are a number of alternatives. The important thing is for every person to have his own, separate home.

●a major concern is making sure the shelters are spread out. To enjoy the benefits -- solitude, quiet, the feeling of one's own place -- each camper must have ample personal space.

sensing walk

●the sensing walk takes place as soon as camp is set up; it is the introduction to an awareness of the place.

●each exercise takes 5 - 10 minutes. Spread the exercises out. There is movement in between, and change of position.

●take plenty of time with your instructions -- give the campers adequate opportunity -- GO SLOWLY -- LISTEN to help you time the next step. See the guidelines for a Quiet Walk. (Use other techniques from the Quiet Walk chapter; many can be used interchangeably.)

●break up the group to walk back to camp alone, using senses, discovering individually.

●a sensing walk is not a hike; the goal is not to cover a great distance geographically, but to open up to what can be found even in a small area.

●for the "negative spaces" exercise, select a tree that's fairly open, that can be seen as a single unit of the forest, with lots of space around it.

tools

●other tools can be made using the jackknife: e.g., a fishing pole and hook.

●have knives, bags, and whetstones prepared. Give them out at the end of the input, not before, or the attention will go from the input to the knives. The knives for this trip are provided. Make it clear ahead of time that sheath knives should be left behind.

●in fact, there are special criteria for tools at Crusoe Camp. There is no axe. A bucksaw, for firewood, is well-cared for and kept off the ground. Each person has a spoon, pierced at the handle, with a leather thong through the hole. Each is responsible for his own, keeping it and washing it. The only other eating utensil is a tin cup. It is surprising to discover how many foods can be eaten with a cup and a spoon! Simple, natural foods and one-pot meals fit the theme of Crusoe Camp.

journal

- journals are pocket-size notebooks that can be easily carried. It helps to have a neat cover -- a drawing of a mushroom, leaves, or an animal. Each comes with a pencil stub -- not a long pencil -- that can be carried easily and sharpened with a jackknife!

- inside the cover, as a frontispiece, have an inscription from ROBINSON CRUSOE. We use this one: "I cannot express what a satisfaction it was to me to come into my old hutch and lie down in my hammock-bed. This little wandering journey, without settled place of abode, had been so unpleasant to me that my own house, as I called it to myself, was a perfect settlement to me compared to that; and it rendered everything about me so comfortable that I resolved I would never go a great way from it again while it should be my lot to stay on the island."

crusoe campfire

- the snack at the beginning of this campfire is goat cheese and apples.

- the reading we use from ROBINSON CRUSOE is taken from the first, three or four pages of the chapter titled, "I Am Very Seldom Idle."

exploration

- set the parameters by marking on the sand map; if you have access to a conch shell horn or a cow horn, great; but it's hard to judge the range of sound, so have a tentative idea of the bounds of exploration.

- the exploration time is a good chance for the campers to make sure their vision spots are not too close together.

gathering

- prepare the birchbark basket and have samples of what can be gathered in your area.

- the inner shoots of cattail are boiled like asparagus; the young shoots of fern ("eagle's claw") can be prepared like broccoli.

- other possibilities for gathering:

  seining -- some hold the seine, some are "beaters;" have a song or chant to keep the rhythm.
  fishing -- poles and hooks can be made with the jackknives.
  berries -- in season, are probably the most fun to gather!
  other wild edibles -- select a few in your area.

- books on wild edibles: see Gibbons, Angier, *et al.*

155

frolic

●DO IT WHEN YOU NEED IT! -- both the input and the frolic itself should be done when energy levels seem high. Let there be frolic -- "Human beings never outgrow the need to play" -- but frolic when it isn't interrupting the flow of another experience.

●there are ingredients for frolic, even though it is a spontaneous experience. There are elements that produce an atmosphere conducive to that spontaneity. Who can resist a rope swing? Once someone discovered a patch of good "sliding mud," it became a recurring frolic! The magical moments are a combination of props and timing. Be attuned to the needs of the campers . . . and your own needs.

●don't forget the little things that contain the magic for frolic. Sometimes it helps to turn into four-year-olds!

relationship

●set aside time each day for the relationship; do it at different times of the day and with different weather conditions.

●think about the criteria for a good relationship. They are the same for a relationship with another person or with a dead stump: spending time together, caring, empathizing, sharing, touching, communicating.

bread making

●have the mechanics down -- know what you're doing. Try baking bread yourself before you try it out there with the campers!

●bake the bread in Dutch ovens -- three round loaves to an oven. Each person has his own loaf. This means you need to take along enough Dutch ovens for all.

●we're now getting involved in having the campers grind some of the grain themselves, using a metate and mano. Just add the cracked wheat to the recipe. It gives the bread a great, crunchy texture!

●we use the top of an overturned canoe, covered with brown paper, for kneading. Every camper makes his own loaf. First, take turns grinding a small bit of wheat. Then mix up the dough, again taking turns. Each person then receives a lump of dough, of his own to knead -- that's his loaf. Chant while kneading.

●take turns "watching" the bread as it rises and bakes. Half can leave to go gathering while the other half stays, and then switch. Let the dough rise once, punch it down, and put it in the Dutch ovens. When it rises again, the ovens go into the coals of the fire.

haiku

●don't be critical. This is not poetry-critic time; it's self-expression and natural awareness. And if someone comes back with a haiku that scans 4-8-5 -- let it be.

156

totem
    campfire

●if there is a snack at the totem campfire, it comes at the beginning where it won't interrupt the mood. And it is a "natural" snack: fruit, nuts, cheese.

●when the input is over, it's time for each to depart for his shelter, instead of lingering around the fire. Tomorrow will be a big day. If you feel the need for a longer campfire, tell the story of a vision quest or the search for a totem.

vision
    quest

●as an alternative to letting them choose their own vision spots if the area is limited, have a half dozen or so sites selected. Lead each to a place blindfolded or in silence or both. That ritual makes it his vision spot.

●the vision quest is not intended to be either religious or supernatural. It is a time to spend in solitude and in one place, to think and feel and absorb.

magic
  circle
    campfire

●to facilitate the workings of the magic circle, the leader may have to intervene, reemphasizing that the focus is on feelings, not thoughts. Stress, "I FEEL . . ."

●one of the reasons we do this is to get away from endless verbalizing; talk is easy, too easy in most cases. But it's hard to put feelings into words. This is quickly learned in a magic circle campfire. It might help to mention that the hardest things to say are often the most important, and vice versa.

●we open up from the magic circle format a little to talk about individual vision quests. Still, the thrust is to discover and express one's own feelings about what happened. When someone begins relating an experience, ask him, "How did you FEEL at that moment?"

●the magic circle campfire does not go on until the wee hours of the morning. After vision quest feelings are shared, the group links up for one more round of the magic circle -- and then each departs for his individual shelter to be alone for the night.

●during all rounds of the magic circle, each person should repeat the words, "This evening, I feel . . ."

MUIR TREK

The whole day was active; one thing led to another. It was sort of "get out and go!" It was fun to do that. Fantastic. First, seeing the eagle, then those suspended spider webs glittering in the morning sunlight. Sloshing in the muck. Eating bread and cheese at "the tree."

You don't have to worry about time -- it just doesn't mean a whole lot. You're out there and you can enjoy yourself and there's nothing you have to do.

It's hard for me to explain why I like wilderness -- I just do. I want to run like the wind, glide like a bird, live like Nature lives, and dies.

Lake was covered with fog. Really cool! Wow! The sun was blazing through fog. Canoers silhouetted against sky! Wow!

I felt that I was coming closer to nature because I wasn't covering it up or tearing it down, but moving with it.

Man invents things to do what he can't do himself -- but it takes all the fun out of it. He builds a car to go faster, but you're all enclosed. You can't feel the speed or the power or the feeling of the movement.

Wondering where a path leads, or what lies beyond the next hill, and going to find out is a Muir Trek; it's also a much longer sailing voyage to an uninhabited island. Often, it is a one-day adventure, from before dawn until slightly after dusk. But this kind of trek can come in many shapes and sizes.

There are several elements which constitute a Muir Trek, and each is a factor in that flexibility. First, the sensation of movement is deeply felt -- walking, bicycling, canoeing, sailing, and horseback riding are the "elemental vehicles," the modes of transportation for the trek. Secondly, there is an atmosphere of enthusiasm and joy surrounding the venture. And finally, the basis for the trek is for a small band of travelers, six adolescents and an adult, to wander through the natural wild places that no one knows.

These needn't be undiscovered places nor virgin wilderness. By "a natural wild place that no one knows," we don't mean only the wilderness of northern Saskatchewan -- although that's part of it. There are many natural wild places closer to home, places that no one really KNOWS. We go seeking beauty in such places, intending to really perceive what others miss.

Traveling in a way that lets us feel, doing sensory exercises that heighten our abilities to perceive, thinking about beauty and our need for it, and stopping to take time to really absorb a scene and to get in touch with the essence of a particular place -- all these are part of the Muir Trek. And that is how we find the natural wild places that no one knows. We get to know them, using all our senses and giving all of ourselves to the effort.

If you think about your muscles, they feel tired. They don't seem to be a part of you, in a way. Most of the time you're taking them for granted -- like something you use a lot. Like a pencil -- it becomes a part of you, it's so natural. But when you really think about holding it, it doesn't seem a part of you anymore. Same thing with other parts of your body.

> MOVEMENT. Sensing motion and focusing on how it feels to our muscles.

"Let's focus for a moment on our bodies and how they feel -- what the muscles are telling us today about how we use our bodies. There are many things we do automatically, without ever feeling what we're doing. Write your name in your sketchbook. . . Did you feel the weight of the pencil in your hand, or feel the muscles in your fingers, hand, and arm? Writing is often one of the automatic things that we do because we are so used to it. But switch the pencil to your other hand -- that hand that isn't used to writing. Write your name with that hand. Do you feel the weight of the pencil now? Think about what your muscles have to do in order to perform just that simple activity, something you usually take for granted. Your canoe paddle is sort of the same way, so when we start canoeing again, feel your muscles moving the paddle through the water.

"To add to your awareness -- to help you focus -- try some stretching exercises. Extend your arms down and slowly bring them way up over your head and around behind you. Do this a couple of times and think about drawing all the environment into you and through you with your movements. Feel your muscles stretching, and kind of stretch the way that feels good to your muscles.

"Now, to wake up one of our senses, and to give some energy to those muscles, I have an orange for each of you. Catch! Feel its weight. Smell it. Rub it along your check. An orange is really like STORED sunshine. When we peel it and eat it, we get the energy. So let's "open" our oranges by peeling the sections back like rays of the sun. The sun gives our muscles energy to move. Think about movement."

The tree was but a little seed, lying in the ground. But this soon changed, and the tree began to sprout . . . It grew and grew and grew, and then it grew some more. The tree grew for some hundred years, and then it grew some more. But then a man, a small, small small man, came walking with his axe. He chopped the tree; he chopped it some more, and fell it to the ground.

LAND. Thinking about the land, what has happened to it, and the effects man has had on it.

"The soil that I am holding was made from rock that was broken up by wind, water and ice, and from plants that lived and died long ago and have been decomposed by tiny animals. Soil. Earth. Land. It takes thousands of years for one inch of soil to form from bare rock.

"Think about what this area looked like without soil. Start by imagining it without trees, without bushes, wildflowers or ferns, without grass. Then peel back the very ground in your imagining, the roots and humus and soil. Underneath that there's probably sand -- and then, way down, there is bare rock. Thousands -- millions of years ago, this was all just rock. Rock and water and air and sunlight. Think of it . . .

"There are a lot of interesting things in the history of the land we're traveling across; like the glaciers and what they did to the area. Everything that's here, really, is a result of the Ice Age. When it came, it really changed this land.

"Man has had some effects here, too. There are no huge old trees here like I've seen in other places. This area was all logged off about eighty years ago and the forest has had to kind of start over again.

"As we go along, let's try to read the landscape and figure out what has happened here. The land has a history, both of natural events and human activity. Let's see if we can find out about some of it. We can try to figure out why it is the way it is, and we can look for things that don't seem to belong -- like a rock jutting up or a sudden open space in the forest. The land is like a special kind of book that can be read only by those who have a certain set of eyeglasses. Let's imagine that we all have a pair of those 'magic' glasses. With them we can see both the past and the future of the land."

162

I feel as though time is moving fast. That I am so far behind and that I will never catch up. But I do. I worry about the future and before I know it the future that I worried about is now my past. Let me move with the present and learn from the past.
Clouds scurrying by,
leaves rustling in the trees,
a feeling of content.

SKETCHBOOK. A record of the impressions, adventures, and essences found on the Muir Trek.

"Your sketchbook is for your use as a tool for self-expression. You can sketch, or write poetry, or keep notes. It's your opportunity to express what you are seeing and feeling on the Muir Trek. On the last trek I did the best sketch I've ever done in my life. I'm not an artist, and I've never really sketched before, but somehow being here and taking it all in helped me be more creative. I was really pleased with what I did, even though someone else might not think it was so good.

"But this is the point of the Muir sketchbook. It's for you to use and to be comfortable with. One of the best ways to look at a place and really see all that's there is to try to sketch it with the most simple of words or lines.

"Like their haiku poetry, the Japanese have a form of painting, called sumi, which tries to capture the essence of a setting using only the most necessary of strokes. In this technique, you sketch with your whole body, not just your hand. Try it . . . Move your whole arm and shoulder . . . Hold your pen loosely . . . It takes only a few strokes to represent nature."

The keyboard of perception -- the different layers. You look at the sky, and the clouds, and get their whole shape in mind, and then the trees, and the line of the horizon behind the trees. And then you just look at the shape of the top against the sky, and look at the clouds. Then you just look at the water, and the line against the shore. Then you take the different layers at separate times and put them all together and then you sort of get a picture of what it's like. Then look away and you can see it -- I mean, you can just SEE it! If you learn the shape of the clouds and the way they are, and then the way the horizon looks, and then the water, and then you close your eyes, you have a really good idea of how it looks! It's really neat!

PERCEPTION. Receiving the world in a fresh, clear way.

"Imagine as you are sitting here, resting, looking out, that you are viewing a canvas, a painting. Look at the scene as an artist might see it. You may even want to use your hands to block out the big groupings, almost like you were painting over the scene. Pick out the major objects: the tree overhanging the water, the lake itself, the trees on the far shore, the sky, the low plants in the foreground. Feel them in space and describe them with your hands. Then trace the major lines: the shore line, the horizon, the straight lines of the trees and the curves of the clouds. Keep these in focus too. As you are looking, keep your eyes moving. Try to expand your peripheral vision, taking in all there is to see. When you have your canvas fully in mind with the groupings, the lines, the wholeness of it; close your eyes and see it in your mind's eye (maybe use your hands to describe it once more in space). Then, when you've reconstructed your canvas and' feel content, open your eyes and look at it again.

"Another thing you can do to heighten your perception is to mentally subtract elements of the scene. For example, look at your canvas and imagine it without color. Imagine it at night when all colors are reduced to black and grey and white. Take away the lighting, the sunshine, to imagine how different the scene would be if it were all in shadow. Or mentally subtract sound. Imagine that it is silent, without the sound of the waves on the shore, or the wind. Take away all movement, all that rippling water in the lake. Imagine it mirror still. By doing this, you focus on some of the things that make this place at this time what it is. This scene is composed of many, many elements, all of which are important in making it itself. All the elements combine to be what you perceive.

"Now is a good time to stretch or sketch if you like; we'll take a break"

Once the stream was so shallow for canoes we got out and decided to walk . . . As soon as people overcame their fear it was fantastic!

It was unbelievable that the beaver can build such a dam. It was about 75 feet long, holding back a two-foot wall of water!

Thinking about sinking waist deep into swamp and mud can provoke pretty negative thoughts. Or so I thought. The feeling of standing waist deep in warm mud and constantly being pulled down is hard to describe, but once you got used to it -- it was fun!

ADVENTURE. Reaching out into the unknown, discovering natural wild places no one knows.

"John Muir was an American naturalist who spent most of his life wandering and moving and exploring. Born here in Wisconsin, he longed to transcend "the beaten charts of human living." He constantly sought the unknown and sometimes the unknowable. He was almost always on the move; seeking out a new mountain to climb, a new journey to take, a new glacier to explore.

"His vision grew with his travels. The more he saw, the wider his knowledge of the world became. Although his consciousness grew to include the trees and mountains of far-off lands and the shores of foreign seas, he also sought and found beauty in small places close to home. He looked for things that other people missed, and he found them. He could not be content to let his life slip by quietly and sedately; he had to see and experience what was in the world. Discovery or adventure, either could have been John Muir's middle name; they were synonymous with his life.

"In a small way, our trek is a reconstruction of that life: "discovering wild places no one knows." We don't have a particular destination in mind. We'll discover our own destination, we'll know it when we find it.

"The Muir Trek is an adventure because about anything can happen and because it's different from what we do most of the time. Adventure is something you kind of have to carve out for yourself. We'll make our own adventure.

"Let's turn the circle outward for a moment, so we're facing all different directions. We're like the points of a compass. There might be an adventure waiting in any of those directions. Going around the circle, each of us can describe what we think might lie over the horizon or beyond the fringe of the forest in the direction we're facing . . . Let's go!"

We woke up our senses one at a time. We looked at very minute things to wake up our sense of sight; we felt a leaf, we laid on our backs and closed our eyes and just listened for a while; we smelled how green everything smelled . . . I felt it -- like to the soles of my feet! I felt the earth beneath me. I felt it with my hands. It was different from anything I'd ever done before. And that was what Muir Trek was -- different from everything else: an adventure. A very cool experience.

ZEST. Supreme energy and vitality, *joie de vivre.*

"I'd like to talk about John Muir again for a moment and mention a particular quality of his -- zest. He loved life, loved living and being. He loved to be outdoors and to explore the wild places. He did it with such gusto and such a complete giving of himself that one person described him as 'the most ALIVE man I ever met!'

"He would climb one mountain, see another in the distance that was higher and set out to climb it without pausing to take a deep breath. Some people thought he was a little crazy, spending his energy climbing and exploring when he could be producing something more concrete. But John Muir's zest for life could not be contained in a normal everyday existence.

"What zest really is, I guess, is a way of approaching life, really getting into it. It's having a deep enjoyment for life, a hearty appetite for living. This morning, when we ate the oranges, we were waking up our sense of taste. Now, let's wake up our appetites for other things by heightening our 'taste' for each in turn. We'll wake up our senses, one at a time, so they can help us get the fullest enjoyment out of being here. First, open your mouths and nostrils and take in a big bite of air and smell it . . . Get down close to the ground and smell that, too. While you're down there, focus on one blade of grass, one insect, or one tiny piece of rock -- something very very small . . . Using your sense of sight, really 'digest' it; take it in and savor it. . . Let's lie on our backs like spokes of a wheel, now, and listen to the flavor of the sounds around us. . . .

"This has really just been the appetizer -- there's so much more to see and hear and smell and taste and feel. Let's go get the main course!"

I could feel that everything that I was seeing and touching was connected. I once stepped on a plant and knocked it over, and I thought of the berries that might come on it that might feed the birds or whatever and the birds would feed another animal. But then again, that I knocked the plant over and killed it would mean it would decay faster and feed the roots of other things . . . But maybe that's not good, because Nature knows how to handle these things, alone.

WHOLENESS. Everything is connected to everything else; nothing exists in isolation.

"When you were perceiving you tried to look at your canvas as a whole and to see all of the scene. Instead of staring at one thing as we have a tendency to do, you kept your eyes moving to expand your vision and see the scene as a whole.

"The world IS a whole. We just happen to perceive or focus on one part of it at a time. Rocks break down into soil that supports mosses and lichen, which break down more of the rock into soil. Plants that have grown from the soil die and decay and are turned back into soil. Tall trees catch and block the sun, and shade-loving trees grow up beneath this canopy. Creeks empty into lakes where water is evaporated into clouds to fall again as rain and run into the creeks. Nature works in cycles -- there are no ends, and no beginnings, just a continuous circle of life, going on and on. Cycles are circles in time. Time passes, and the cycles just keep repeating themselves. And the cycles connect all life on earth together, like a giant web around the 'globe,' a web that is made of delicate strands woven in an amazingly complex pattern. Life exists within this web, and cannot exist without it, just as it cannot exist without the thin film of life-supporting air that we call the earth's atmosphere. Just think, beyond that film of life, two miles up or a mile or so beneath the sea, there are no plants, no animals, no microbes -- no living things. But within that film there is life that is all inter-woven and made whole by the strands of the web.

"Just as you saw your scene as a whole, and as you begin to see the world as a whole, try to see YOURSELF as fitting in to the unity of nature. To become one with the natural world is not just to see the wholeness. It is to BE, to recognize one's place in that whole -- to stand as a brother with the stones and trees."

I thought about what he was telling us -- that sometimes we take nourishment for granted. Sometimes we nourish ourselves wrongly -- in all ways, not just eating. Sometimes we take all types of nourishment for granted. I think I felt the need for the essence of my little place out there. It was a big log, and there were two sticks across it, and there was moss covering the whole thing, like a log cabin. I kind of felt the need for that kind of cooperation.

NOURISHMENT. Receiving what we need from our environment.

"You know, we take for granted the fact that we eat three times a day. It is necessary to nourish our bodies so that we stay healthy and strong. But how often do we think of our other requirements for nourishment? Like our need for beauty, for awareness, for peace?

"We do have needs other than just our normal body needs -- needs for security, love, respect and our own growth. Yet the needs we systematically think about and structure our society around are the need to eat regularly . . . and perhaps the need to sleep.

"Being out here nourishes me. If I go too long without being outside and in the natural world, I really get to feeling bad. Being here is part of my nourishment, and it helps me stay healthy and happy. This flower is part of my nourishment; it feeds my appetite for beauty, my sense of smell, my sight.

"So take a moment and think about your own individual needs and what nourishes them and perhaps how in your life you can move toward having the full nourishment YOU need."

It was all good, but the thing that made it really great was the celebration. All we did was we just found a nice spot, then we did the flower exercise. I felt myself blowing in the wind just like a flower would. Before -- before I did that -- I was thinking I could do this any day -- but that was the thing that brought it up, that simple little thing. Celebrating -- being in the wilderness. Enjoying being in the wilderness. And not being in a way that was forced on us or that we didn't enjoy.

CELEBRATION. The reverence and respect and joy of life all rolled into one.

"Celebration is kind of giving yourself to the spirit of an event. Think of times that are happy -- times of celebration -- your birthday or a holiday. Some people really get into the spirit of a holiday -- and they're the ones who really enjoy it.

"There are a lot of ways of celebrating, but they all have one thing in common -- you have to really get into it! Remember the flower that you smelled earlier? Let's celebrate the growth of that flower by putting ourselves into its place.

"Instead of thinking like a human being, begin to think of yourself as a plant. And what I'd like you to do is celebrate the flower's birthday by growing and blossoming as it did, expressing plant-likeness with your body. You've received water, and here we are in a sunny spot, standing on good soil. You have all the things a plant needs to grow and bloom. You are a plant. Starting in a crouch, all pulled in tight like a seed, come up slowly. Open up . . . stretching your arms out slowly . . . blooming . . . reaching for light and sun . . .

"Celebrate being alive!"

We set out, paddling into the bank of fog. Slowly each canoe in front of us was engulfed. Then we, too, were surrounded by the fog. It was an eerie feeling, sitting on the lake with everything from the outside world cut off by the fog . . . The mist clung to my body and the mist tickled my lungs, and a bit of nature and the world around me was implanted in my brain. Wow!

> ECSTASY. Losing self-consciousness in a total absorption in Nature.

"Sometimes when you're viewing a scene or listening to a beautiful piece of music -- or sensing anything that you really enjoy -- you become so totally involved with the elements of the experience that you stop thinking about yourself. You become part of what you're experiencing. It just flows into you, and you flow into it. It starts with a sort of tingling mellowness. You feel it welling up inside you, and when you feel it you stay with it, follow it -- flow with it. And that's ecstasy.

"You can't make it happen, but you can prepare yourself for it and open yourself up to it. In fact, ecstasy has something to do with being ready for it -- being on edge and anticipating. And being open to letting it engulf you. Letting it happen.

"What I want to do now is a way of opening up to ecstasy. Maybe nothing will happen -- but maybe this will help you begin to feel the mellowness:

Sit or lie down in a comfortable position . . . close your eyes and let your breathing settle into its own rhythm . . . when you are relaxed, begin to picture in your mind a beautiful sunset . . . you are sitting somewhere, watching that sunset . . .

Explore the area where you are sitting -- what you are sitting on -- what is near you . . . now look again at the sunset . . . explore it in your mind . . . see its colors . . . move into the sky . . . wander in and out among the clouds . . . touch them.

Now, come back to the place where you were sitting before . . . focus on the sunset again . . . as you watch it, it grows larger . . . you become smaller and smaller . . . you are a tiny speck, watching it . . . it draws you toward it, very slowly . . . closer and closer . . . until you become part of the sunset. Now, slowly pull away from the sunset . . . until you are back in your spot here in the circle again . . . just sit quietly for a while . . . until you feel like opening your eyes."

Lying here alone in the grass. All I can see is grass, sky and trees. All I can hear are birds, bugs, and animals. Had to cross the creek to get here -- that kind of adds to the privacy. Things take on a new dimension when being looked at from below up -- blossoms on the grass look like the top branches of a tall tree. Lying down, the grass feels like a feather pillow as it conforms to the shape of my body. Some insect -- probably a grasshopper -- is making noise nearby.

ESSENCE. Distilling the spirit of a wild place.

"What I'd like for you to do now is take about half an hour to yourselves. Find a good spot that you like, your 'essence spot,' and spend some time there with your sketchbook. The purpose for this is to feel the essence of this one particular place you have chosen.

"There are many things you can do. One thing you might do is become like an empty vessel, emptying yourself of all concepts, labels, and thoughts to let this place come to you, fresh and un-conceptualized. You can also empathize with your spot -- try to feel and absorb its particular mood. Another thing you may want to do is just listen. Everything has its own sound; listen to the sounds of your place. They, too, tell a story about it.

"Another approach is to get a different vantage point of your place. Climb a tree and look down at it. Or get down low and see it through the grasses. See it from many different angles. And, finally, you can step back and maybe feel the subtle spirit of this place at this time -- the 'here and nowness' of it. In all the world there is this place, unique and special. And the time is now. It is changing. Perhaps a mushroom that was here yesterday was eaten by an animal, or perhaps tomorrow a tree may fall over into the spot. It is just like this for only a short while. So perceive the mystery of this place and this moment in the wide eternal worlds of time and space.

"This might be a good time to use your sketchbooks, too, to try to capture the essence of this place -- so that when you are gone from it, you will still remember it.

"Essence."

I love to be out in the wilderness, and when I saw those beer cans I felt like picking them up. But I knew if I started, I couldn't pick them all up. Maybe I should have picked up the ones I could. But the whole thing strengthened my idea of the wilderness and how much I enjoy it and like to be in it. I wasn't thinking much about other places, just about that spot, and how much nicer it would have been if they weren't there.

> CONSERVATION. The preservation of our natural communities -- for the use and enjoyment of people for all time.

"John Muir was deeply concerned about conserving our natural resources. He roamed the virgin slopes of mountains in California for ten years. When he returned years later to find the grasses beaten and eaten by livestock, the land parcelled up and the great trees coming down, he was sick with misery. He wrote tirelessly and lectured widely on the evils of forest destruction.

"Look around at this community. Now, picture it without trees -- or without water. How would it look with huge pits dug for mining? What if a road or a power line came right through where you are now sitting? What would happen to this community if any of these things took place?

"The battle that John Muir fought is still continuing. Many people still look at a tree as raw board feet; they don't see its aesthetic beauty. Financial interests and big business want land, trees, and water for their own use and profit; they don't see them as parts of a larger whole. We can only tamper so much with the intricate mechanism of the forest community before we destroy the very COMMUNITY that assures us of the land and trees and water.

"Many people believe these resources should be preserved, should be used sparingly and for the benefit of ALL, and that some land should be left untouched as a haven for animals as well as people. We as individuals have needs other than the material needs of our bodies. Perhaps our society should recognize the value of these communities for nourishing the needs for beauty, for quiet, for nature. And perhaps, too, we should learn to recognize that the greatest resource in the forest is not the lumber; it is the forest COMMUNITY itself, the combination of plants and animals that keep the forest going.

"Part of the land, I feel, should be left untouched by the heavy hand of man -- left in its fresh beauty -- just as it is, and if we are lucky, as it ever shall be. So that there will always be a few wild places for people -- like you -- to be young in."

I think there will always be. wild places, but eventually they'll all be discovered and roamed through. The areas will get less and less. If no one's been there before, you know there's nothing out there, you don't have to worry about anybody or anything. If people have canoed by and not gotten out, I think that would count as not being there, because they really didn't get out and explore like you would be doing.

REFLECTION. Seeing an image in a clear surface, or taking time to pause and consider what has_ happened.

"Take a moment here to lie down and look at your reflection in the water. What you see isn't really your face. It's an image, a reflection of your face, not the real thing. And in a way, remembering a person you've met or a place you've been is like that. You don't remember the real thing, the face or the scene, but you DO have an image in your mind that is a reflection of the real.

"Remember when you could close your eyes and revisualize your canvas? That was a reflection, an image that you held in your mind. So perhaps, leaving here, we can take a reflection of what we've seen. There is really a kind of double meaning in reflection: it is the image remembered in the mind; it's also taking time to reflect, to think about what has happened. We have wandered through some beautiful land, seen what man has done to the land in some places, found, each of us, a place to be alone and to perceive fully, and thought about what could happen to all of this to destroy it.

"Let's take a little time to be by ourselves -- for reflection."

John Muir pioneered the idea of setting aside land to be preserved for all time as National Parks. What an immense, important, significant idea in the history of America! Too often, we tend to think of a country's greatness as lying in its military might, Gross National Product, or material standard of living. John Muir believed differently. Perhaps it is time for all of us to be more aware of what a country is doing to nourish the growth of consciousness, the awareness of beauty, and the development of gentleness and harmony as an equal part of providing for the basic needs of people.

The National Parks, thanks to John Muir, acknowledge the realization that these factors, too, are important. In addition to providing valuable watersheds and wildlife sanctuaries, the parks are places where souls can be refreshed and renewed.

So John Muir inspired a Muir Trek -- a wandering style of journeying through some of the natural wild places that no one knows. The trek is flexible in time and vehicle; the uniqueness comes from the Muir-inspired qualities of zest, celebration, and becoming one with nature. There is joy and adventure in "trekking." It is almost a Dionysian pilgrimage to honor the nature gods who dwell in the wild places. The emphasis is NOT on miles travelled, nor on having the latest and best equipment, nor even on the quantity or rarity of wildlife seen. There is no destination but this: to SEE and ABSORB a natural wild place that no one knows. The goal is an internal one, to be conscious and joyful in being outdoors and having fun -- and not with beer bottles and baseball and popcorn, although those have their places. The Muir Trek is simply opening oneself to the "virtue of sun and the spirit of air."

And when we begin to feel that consciousness growing, and find ourselves being filled with the sun and air and water and soil and life all around us, we try to capture the essence of that place and that feeling.

There are all kinds of ways to try to record these thoughts, feelings, and sensations: every person can do it -- you don't have to be quote talented unquote. All you really have to do is perceive beauty -- appreciate beauty -- reach out to beauty.

It was Aldo Leopold -- another important man in the history of America's environmental awareness -- who said: "I am glad I shall never be young without wild country to be young in. Of what avail are forty freedoms without a blank spot on the map?" No one would have agreed more readily than John Muir. His soul needed the wild places, and he wanted the generations which would succeed him to have those benefits, too. So that is another reason for Muir Trek -- to share with at least one more generation an opportunity to be young in a wild country. There may not be many more chances.

John Muir never followed a planned itinerary -- neither do we, except for the considerations of the camp structure. Muir took children to the woods for spontaneous botanizing -- we hope to perpetuate that spontaneity. John Muir roamed far and wide enjoying nature, encouraging other people to do so, and working to preserve and conserve wild places everywhere -- and we follow in his footsteps, trying our hardest to keep up!

general
- for openers, plan a one-day trip to leave before dawn and return after sundown.

- prepare and pack the essentials for the trip beforehand, so that this doesn't have to be done in the pre-dawn hours!

- be sure participants get to bed early the night before so they can enjoy the beauties of a pre-dawn setting. Have them lay out their clothes, "fireman style" for a quick and silent departure.

- awaken them yourself in the morning, keeping the tone hushed and quiet, not disturbing others.

- use simple sidepacks for shared lunch items, raingear, sketchbook and pencils; we carried plastic canteens on web belts. The leader should carry a first aid kit, making sure to check ahead of time on the medical status of the campers going.

- for hiking, make a pre-trek shoe-check! Also, each person should have a suitable hat and poncho.

- food: we emphasize natural foods. For the movement input, and as an early morning breakfast, oranges; brunch is muffins and honey and "gorp" (granola, raisins, peanuts, M&M's); lunch is French bread, a variety of cheeses, apples, and water.

- there are many possible modes of transportation, all of them "elemental vehicles:" hiking, canoes, horseback, sailing, bicycles. For winter trekking -- snowshoes or cross-country skis are possibilities.

- all inputs are done in a circle.

- there is no set destination and there are no watches.

movement
- the Muir Trek leaves before dawn, so that it is enroute when the sun rises; there's magic in that. This input on movement is done after about an hour of travel, at an early stop, perhaps just after the sun has risen.

- during the pencil and stretching exercises, allow plenty of time for individual differences.

- demonstrate how to peel the orange like rays of the sun. Make vertical cuts -- like the longitudinal lines on a globe -- around the orange. Peel the "petals" back, one at a time. Then eat the orange, slowly -- one section at a time -- savoring each section.

sketchbook
- have the sketchbooks prepared in advance. These should be small enough to be easily handled and large enough to accommodate sketching. We cut large sketchpads into two 5" x 10" sketchbooks.

- the sketchbooks should have simple covers -- tagboard covered with a plain, coarse fabric. Instead of a frontispiece quotation, try an example of sumi painting.

land
- SOIL LIVES! It is important that you don't convey the idea that you are holding just dead things. There are millions upon millions of living, single-celled plants and animals in a handful of rich soil.

perception
- it doesn't have to be a "postcard vista." One of the key points of the Muir Trek is that beauty can be perceived anywhere.

- when going through the exercise, watch the timing. Take your time -- give them time -- and GO SLOWLY!

adventure
- keep the "compass point" descriptions fairly brief, but allow room for imaginations to grow and build.

- there are many elements that make up adventure: one of them is the "risk" factor. This can, however, be minimized. Remember, too, that because adventure means breaking out of standard habit patterns and even common day-to-day behavior, there is a self-esteem risk in adventure -- doing the unusual.

- although there isn't a set destination, there probably is a definite time for the return. There should also be a rough idea of the area through which you will be wandering. (Even though you have to be back at a certain time, it can be a loose, easy trek if you de-emphasize the necessity of returning. Live in the here and now for as long as possible!)

- for a fascinating account of John Muir's life, see *Son of the Wilderness.*

zest
- go through the exercises slowly.

- be zestful yourself on the Muir Trek. Zest is pzazz, sparkle, vitality, relish. Put yourself into it. If the leadership doesn't sparkle, the input on zest is useless!

wholeness
- when you speak of the world being whole, form the "earth" circle with your hands. Put your thumbs with their tips touching and with the fingers of each hand close together; touch the index and middle fingers together. The thumbs form the lower half of the circle, the fingers form the "northern" hemisphere.

nourishment
- after speaking of the flower and before closing the input, pass the flower around for everyone to smell and to brush against their cheeks. Then pause -- give them time to think about their needs. Count to 200 without saying anything.

- this input would best follow a snack-break.

177

celebration •this is a sort of "mini-celebration." It may spark other, spontaneous celebrations later in the day. Great!

ecstasy •go through the exercise slowly. Insert long pauses between the phrases (. . .) give them a chance to become involved. And at the end, just remain silent until all eyes are open.

•don't force involvement -- perhaps note at the beginning that if someone doesn't want to do this, or at any point feels like stopping, he should just open his eyes and remain sitting quietly.

•the pause before the "pulling away" should be long, perhaps over a minute. Then, when you begin speaking again, use a slightly louder tone.

•the trek will last until after sunset, so the campers will have a chance to see a sunset; having already thought about it and built up to it, they may indeed experience total involvement. But don't YOU say anything about it. In this case, you have to let them let it happen.

essence •set up parameters, depending on the area: how far to go, avoiding safety hazards, etc.

•have a pre-arranged signal for the return: a whistle, a horn, an animal call.

conservation •when asking the questions, leave time for thinking and reflecting. That is, after all, the purpose of the questions.

•on the entire trek, point out examples of "man and his land" -- the different ways in which man affects his environment. Not all are bad. Many are ill-planned. Focus on what man has done to the land.

•make sure that the Muir Trek does not violate its own values; pack out all potential pollutants. And in the natural wild place, emphasize that man can enjoy the community without destroying it. The hand of man can be gentle as well as heavy -- touch, but not break.

reflection •if there is no calm body of water, put water in a metal basin. Or ask, "Have you ever seen your reflection in a pool of water?"

•the ideal time for the reflection would be about sunset; so that each can view this daily phenomenon alone, in silence. Spend about half an hour for this time, if possible. Have a pre-arranged signal for the regrouping or keep the parameters small.

178

ACCLIMATIZING IS . . .

SETON JOURNEY

We were walking up the second highest point on the mountain. It was really steep and really high and we were all really tired. Then we got to the top, and it was really worth it! We could see practically the whole island. We saw the biggest island on the biggest lake in North America! We felt on top of the world when we were up there . . .

It poured all day; however, we did not stop hiking. We got to Todd Harbor, waterlogged. Everyone pitched in and we set up three tarps, collected firewood (somewhat wet) and started dinner. We went to bed, wet but expecting, hoping for, a day of sunshine. . . .

The next morning, after a sound sleep, we got up, had breakfast and then a seed. We left rather quickly. It was a beautiful day -- the sun was hot and the breeze was cool. The excitement was rolling through our bones. I watched the gulls, and all they do is float. Not moving a muscle.

There are only a few places in this country where one can walk for a day without finding a road. Isle Royale is one of them. The only way to cross the interior of the island is to walk. So six young people and an adult don backpacks and set out for a ten-day walk down the fifty-mile length of the Greenstone Ridge.

Careful preparations are made to check equipment and supplies. And just as carefully, a series of focal points and inputs are developed, to maximize the experience of ten days and to enhance the enjoyment and awareness of each of those days. The inputs make Seton Journey more than a backpacking trip. The goal is not to prove one's stamina and endurance. The hiking is not an end in itself, and the purpose does not lie in reaching the other end of the island.

Walking is the mode of transportation which allows us to reach our real goal, a close-up view of this incredibly beautiful wilderness. Walking helps attain this goal, not only because it is necessary, but because of its inherent rhythm, simplicity, and naturalness. Walking contributes to the journey the feeling of moving with nature. Walking, one can follow animals, stop to sit quietly and observe, look at the sky, listen to the sounds, and reach out to touch the beauty -- and be touched by it.

The Seton Journey is ten days of walking without rigid time schedules. It is time to be aware, to enjoy, to appreciate, and to marvel at what can be seen and heard in this unspoiled land: the chance sightings of moose, the scampering of a red squirrel across the trail, or the magnificent ridge-top views. The real purpose of a Seton Journey is natural observation in its deepest and fullest sense.

Perhaps the tone of the journey can best be set by the words which begin Harry's journal, the thoughts of the leader who will share that tone with the young people:

"23 July, 1973. Sitting in my cabin the night before Seton Journey. I've just said goodbye to my friends and feel left alone suddenly -- like it's all up to me now.

"I feel like the trip will be totally unexpected. We've planned a general itinerary, where we are going basically -- and have sufficient food and gear -- yet besides these two 'knowns', destination and provisions, all that we see and experience is going to be unexpected.

"Maybe general knowledge, like 'we'll see wildlife' and we'll be hiking and focusing on nature, ourselves, and simplicity. But mostly -- all will be new. That's a really nice feeling.

"I guess my whole feeling at this moment is centered on that unknown experiencing we'll do. I'm not worried about food or gear or packs, or much of anything about how it will go. It will be okay and I'll do my best.

"I wonder what we'll see."

July 24 (Rock Harbor) -- After a long, often tedious journey on the Ranger III, I am now on edge with anticipation, waiting to plunge into the wilderness with 1 (ONE!) backpack. The concrete banks of Rock Harbor don't harbor any thoughts worth writing about, so I won't write anything more. But one observation: that feeling of a great trip just starting is not comparable to any other sensation. "My bags are packed, I'm ready to go." Charge!

COOPERATION. Helping each other out, being aware of others and thinking of their welfare as well as one's own.

"If we cooperate, we're going to have a good time here -- even if we're rained on and we run out of food and we don't see one single animal the entire trip -- because we will have a bond of caring for each other, and that will sustain us. We will have shared with each other the joys and sorrows of the whole experience.

"If we don't cooperate, if we are selfish and greedy and if we think only of ourselves -- even if it is a super trip in other ways -- it will be a failure in my mind because we haven't cared about each other.

"Camping out together for ten days asks cooperation from all. Everyone must give. Different people have different things to give, but each has something. Cooperation also means accepting the gifts of others. Helping another guy put up his shelter, waiting your turn for dinner, anticipating another's need, sharing food, regulating your pace, checking on the trail to be sure all are well, taking your turn cheerfully at cooking and cleaning: these are some of the cooperations of a Seton Journey.

"And at the end -- if we do cooperate -- there will be a really warm feeling among us all. If we don't care about each other, there's going to be just a gnawing, cold emptiness.

"Let's stand up together now, with our hands still linked. Cooperation -- helping each other up."

There were some stretches of forest that were just like tunnels. They were just so dense that where the path went through it was like a tunnel. Off the trail, it was like it was untouched by anything. Just preserved there. I don't think anyone would walk off the trail. It was like everything was untouched . . . That's what it's all about, really, this trip -- nature.

Things aren't beautiful the way most people think of beauty -- beauty in appearances. Moose aren't really beautiful in appearance, but in their own way, they're beautiful. Beautiful as a MOOSE.

While I'm sitting here writing this I can hear the rush of the lake and the cry of the sea gull.

NATURAL OBSERVATION. Taking time to perceive and wonder about the natural world.

"Natural observation is as natural as breathing. As we walk, just as a matter of course, we check out the forest, the sky, the plants, the unexpected things that come along. Natural observation is all that we do with our senses, all our contacts with our environment. Nothing is so simple, yet so complex; so easy, yet so important. Our whole goal in hiking is to give us a chance to see the natural world up close. And so we go with nothing but a backpack, and we walk to immerse ourselves in the natural environment.

"Everyone turn around and face outward. Each of you can now make a simple natural observation to share with the group . . . What do you see?

"Natural observations are all around you -- all of the time. We observe many things as we hike, but at least once a day, we'll take time to focus on what's going on in one area. During these times you can ask yourself questions about why a plant has grown a certain way or why an animal prefers living in one particular spot. Wonder about what is happening to the plants, the animals, the way land is being formed. Gather information about your surroundings -- and record your questions and observations in your log just as Ernest Thompson Seton did before you.

"Let's pause now and try this for a while. There's a lot to see -- all you have to do is look. Let Nature speak to you."

July 25 -- the birch were high and thin and we could just barely see the waters of Lake Superior. We went on farther and just as we turned a corner, over to our left we saw a big moose. We watched him a second and went on. Then all of a sudden we saw another one. We stopped. Then when we proceeded, another appeared with antlers about four feet wide! There we were, standing in the rain, getting wet and having a staring contest with three bull moose. It was like we were staring at a wall. It's like the moose were saying, "Where do you think you are? This is our land." We were as strange to them as they were to us. But they didn't really care about us, so they turned and left and we went on.

LOG. An individual record of the thoughts and experiences and observations of the Seton Journey.

"Ernest Thompson Seton always carried a notebook along on his travels to record his observations. In his log he kept notes on animal behavior and he sketched pictures of what he saw. He mused about why men killed wolves and why they then created untrue stories about the savagery of wolves. He followed ducks through a swamp, recording their feeding habits, movements, and mating patterns. He noted the plants and animals of many areas.

"All the intimate things he learned about wild creatures he wrote down -- to weave later into books like *Wild Animals I Have Known* and *Lives of the Hunted*. The sketches he kept or developed into paintings. And it must have been a joy for him to come back from journeys and return to the natural logs, to relive those experiences in the wild.

"And this is what the Seton Log is for. It is for your use -- for recording, drawing, and thinking. Take it with you on your natural observation times. Try sketching a wildflower that you find. Trying to draw it can help you observe how it grows. Jot down things you see and things that happen, so when you get back you can remember them. Your Seton Log is your record of the journey."

We walked with the trees and bushes rubbing against our legs. We traveled on foot. Like an animal. Not by car, or by artificial means. The packs on our backs were our portable life. We used the trees as walls and the sky as a roof. The whole concept of being close to nature was brought out. We sweat the land. We wore blisters on our feet as we walked the land. Everything became more and more real.

WALKING. The most elemental way to travel; we can use our legs to get us where we want to go.

"The worn path which runs through our circle has been made by many feet, walking here just as we are doing. Think about the thousands of feet, the millions of steps, that are a part of this trail. And then think that the Indians, long ago, had hundreds of paths like this that crossed vast stretches of the continent -- thousands of miles of paths, and walking, took them where they needed to go.

"The whole Seton Journey is walking. Only it isn't just walking -- it's WALKING. It's important. We need our legs. We need their sturdiness and their rhythmic motion to move us down the island on this path. Walking fifty miles is much different than driving a car fifty miles. It will take us about a week to walk our journey. We'll see moose and squirrels and eagles -- get thirsty, sweat, feel tired, rest -- climb rocks and explore caves, sometimes jump and run down hills -- watch the sun make its daily journey through the sky, see the stars at night -- be awakened by animals feeding in the creek -- get rained on and then feel the joy of the next day being sunny and bright -- climb a ridge to see the whole green virgin island plus the U.S. on one side and Canada on the other, both miles away over blue water. If you could drive a car here, you'd make it in an hour and you'd just see some trees whizzing by.

"So we walk, carefully: sometimes slowly, poking and meandering, sometimes really 'trucking' to make our campsite. And we feel good at the end of the day, because our bodies have had healthy exercise and our senses have received beauty from the island.

"As we move on, think about how you walk. Do you lean into it, or are you letting your feet lead? Feel your muscles working -- stretching -- growing stronger. Walking."

July 27—Surprising enough, I awakened on my own accord feeling rested and refreshed. I got up and proceeded to start a fire for breakfast and get out the necessary food, for I was one of the two breakfast men. I was one of the first ones up. Soon I washed up and breakfast was begun. It was foggy and a bit chilly.

MORNING RITUAL. The washing of hands, face, and neck with water in the morning -- a short, but meaningful "waking up" ceremony.

"Where possible on the Seton Journey, we'll have morning rituals. When we're near a lake or have plenty of water available, it really feels good to me to just silently spend some time waking up with water.

"I splash it on my face five or six times -- let it run down my neck and in my ears. I wash my hands -- and if I'm really feeling brave I take off my shirt and splash my chest. (Should my energy level be just bursting at the brim, I may plunge all the way in!) And that's why each of you has a bandana or soft tool like this one. If you always carry it with you -- hanging from your back pocket or tied around your neck -- then it's always available as a small towel.

"And if there's no lake, but we have enough water, we'll fill this basin for our morning ritual. When water is scarce, a few drops to moisten the bandana will do.

"It may seem simple, but if you try it and really feel it, it works. I can go down to the lake blurry-eyed and foggy and by just taking that time to wash and splash, come back ready to go and feeling very good inside, awake and ready to live the day to the fullest!

"Part of it is doing the morning ritual silently, alone, and sensing the water. Part of it is just the cold water on the face. And part of it is magic."

I like to look at clouds for what they aren't instead of what they are. Sometimes they look like animals -- they aren't, but that's the thing about clouds. If you don't look, you don't see it. In this busy, hustling world, you just have to stop. Nobody can impress that on anybody enough. That's why I came here.

Nature makes her own rules, and as long as you stick to not interrupting it, you're not breaking the rules.

RHYTHMS. The flow of the day in the environment and in our· bodies.

"As we sit here, let yourself become aware of your heartbeat . . . Feel it pulsing and pushing the blood through your body with each stroke. Listen for the sound it makes, unlike anything else, deep in your chest.

"And listen to your breathing, the air coming in and then going out; listen, and feel it, too.

"These rhythms are going on inside us all the time, even though we are usually unaware of them. Another body rhythm we have is waking in the morning and going to bed at night. Another is eating and excreting. Our body is a biological organism full of rhythms, the rhythms of life. Think about rhythms in our life here. Often, human beings pattern their daily lives artificially, by a clock: eating at certain hours -- maybe even looking at a clock to see whether they CAN eat lunch yet; sleeping when it is time, not when they are tired.

"On Seton Journey, the rhythms of our bodies and of the sun will determine our patterns of living. We'll rest when our bodies are tired, drink when we need the water, and decide to eat when we are hungry. We'll be tired at the end of the day, and without electricity we'll sleep when the sun goes down. And the sun will wake us in the morning.

"There are many rhythms in the natural world: the coolness in the morning when the sun is not quite up; the increasing warmth of mid-day with its heat and laziness and time to slow down a bit; afternoon breezes and the day begins to fade -- then evening and sunset when it draws to a close. Night brings darkness, stars, the moon. The earth is full of rhythms; so are all the animals. So are we."

It felt good. You had everything on your back that you needed. It was really kind of cool. Everything there, on your back. It seems like at home for ten days you have a big house -- and that's pretty hard to put on your back! Water, clothes, food. Shelter, too. Your home -- everything on your back -- walking through Isle Royale. You feel proud of yourself. It's really kind of a self-sufficiency.

It's like sorting through your belongings and realizing there are things you'd like to have but that they're luxuries -- you don't need them.

SIMPLICITY. With only the barest essentials we experience the natural world.

"It's really kind of a neat feeling to know that you've got everything on your back. You do of course still need light and air and water and the earth, but your physical comforts -- all your personal needs -- are all there in a fairly small self-contained pack that you carry. It's really incredible when you think about it.

"Our life on the trail is simple, too. We hike, looking at what we see, finding and exploring interesting things. Unfettered by time or demands or expectations. Someone has said it: 'The less that stands between you and the environment, the more aware you will be of it.' We can experience just BEING when we're here. Life is simple and basic and good. Let's go experience it!"

It feels good having the weight on your back, but it is a bit straining. The strain of carrying the pack is there when IT'S there, but it leaves right away. It's the neatness of being here that sort of moves the strain out of the way. And just the whole idea of carrying your home on your back moves the strain out of the way, too. And you really feel aware of your body. For every gain, there's a loss -- for every loss, there's a gain. If your feet hurt, that's the loss -- but you gain being here. It's a good pain. It's worth it.

CARE FOR YOURSELF. Learning to care for your own body -- sense its needs and fulfill them.

"Cleaning your fingernails seems like a little thing, but it can make you feel better about yourself. You're taking care of yourself -- caring for your body. And that's important.

"On the Seton Journey, you guys take care of yourselves. I'm here to help and to guide and to make sure everything is smooth, but most of what is done is done by you yourselves. No one else can carry your pack down the island. No one else will set up your shelter -- unless two of you decide to cooperate and set up two together. No one else will fix a meal that you are responsible for. And no one else will know your home on your back and how to care for it in an orderly way. All this is up to you.

"Oh, we'll help each other out. That's a big part of the trip, too; we have on Seton a strong blend of cooperation AND self-reliance. Both are essential. You really must be pretty well able to take care of yourself before you can genuinely reach out and help someone else. This trip, hopefully, by its very nature will help you become more aware of how important it is -- and also how really good it feels -- to take care of yourself."

We took a couple of trails, just carrying our lunch, and we did a lot of things along the way. We stopped and seton-watched; we looked around a lot more -- had our heads up a lot more. We saw birds, and we saw a few snakes -- snakes aren't usually seen out here. We stopped once on the trail though, for lunch, and we had a red squirrel just come out of the trees and walk right around us! We were really quiet. All along the trail, we didn't talk much at all.

PACE. The rate of walking, the speed at which we move.

"Everybody unlace your right boot . . . It's something you would usually do rather quickly, routinely. Now, lace it back up, but do it VERY SLOWLY, really paying attention to every motion you make doing it -- every detail of the action. Be aware of the pace -- the speed -- at which you're doing this very simple thing.

"I think here on Seton more than anywhere else, you will be aware of the pace of your walk. Some of you walk faster than others; some like to hurry, and some like to sort of amble along. Try different paces and see how they feel. Really take off 'trucking' and see if it's exhilarating or exhausting or both. Or just meander and poke and find out if you see more and feel better, or if you just start thinking about catching up.

"You know we all have our pace of living as well as our pace of walking. And even that pace varies. I'm usually a fairly slow-moving person. I like to take my time and not get hassled or rushed. But if I'm excited or happy -- or just want to clean house before I go outside -- I go lickety-split and get the job done. And that feels good, too.

"Think about your own life pace. Does it feel good in general? And are you content with it? A city pace is generally fast, a wilderness pace is generally slow. What is nature's pace -- or does it vary? Think about your pace."

We went for a hike to Huginnin Cove. We did the circle: 5 miles there, 3 1/2 miles back. Huginnin Cove is one of the most extraordinary places I've ever been to. Sea gulls were all over. Big Rocks. Trees. And the ridge was staring you in the eye, the ridge we had to come over to get to the cove. The sky was royal blue with an occasional cloud. The water was emerald green and turquoise. Wavy and rushing towards the rocks. Splashing, washing, and wonderfully wet against rock and face. Just couldn't get enough!

> ENERGY. The capacity to live, to move about, to do meaningful things.

"The food we eat is turned into energy by our bodies -- the energy which we need to hike the length of this island. Have you noticed the enormous swings in the amount of energy available to you? Out here, without distractions, and being pretty active, you can really feel your body's energy.

"Be aware of how it feels to get up in the morning, refreshed and hungry if you've had a good, deep sleep; or disturbed and restless if you haven't slept well. Breakfast gives more energy, and we're on the trail. The energy of our bodies enables us to hike for miles. Maybe we get fatigued and take a break, a lunch stop: resting in the sun, relaxing and renewing our bodies' energy with food. After lunch, how strong we feel! Ready again to hike with vigor. And at evening, there is time to relax and slow down. More food at dinner and then we sit around a bit and really feel our bodies. their fatigue and need for rest. Then to bed, finally, and the cycle repeats itself.

"The plants have used energy from the sun to make the food we eat; the food, combining with the air we breathe and the water we drink, becomes energy again for our bodies' use. Energy from the world comes into our bodies and is transformed through us into the Seton Journey, hiking fifty miles down this island. No energy lost or gained -- just changed, from sunlight and food and water and air into an incredible experience for us all."

The day before was really hot -- we were saying, "Water! water! water!" But you never wanted to see heat or fire more in your life than today. One day you wish for one thing, the next day you wish for just the opposite. We collected water -- it was really a gift to have rain water. Water -- wow. Sometimes when we stop and drink a little bit of water, I can feel it all the way down, cold and wet, and almost hear it splash at the bottom! We're really learning how precious water is.

> WATER. The miracle resource we take for granted so much of the time.

"On the island, we have to boil water before we can drink it. It has been contaminated, not by man, but by animals and the parasites that live in them. Boiling all the water we drink takes time and effort; but, even though this is a deprivation of sorts, it can remind us of the preciousness of water.

"Sixty-five per cent of our own body is composed of water. And without fresh water to drink, man could not survive for more than a few days. Since water is limited here, we are careful with it: not spilling, not wasting.

"The island also is supported and surrounded by water. Here we can swim, cleanse ourselves and renew our water supply. Think of the water coming down as rain from the sky; water which makes all life possible, water for trees to grow tall and green, cool water to balance the heat of the sun, and more water to drink. Think about the water returning to the sky as it evaporates from the lakes, the ground, the plants, and our own bodies; forming into clouds, then falling again as rain. And think about the 'invisible' water all around you: in the air, in the soil, in the plants, and again, in your body -- or how much water was used in making all of your clothing and equipment. It took several gallons of water just to make your shoes!

"And each time you raise your canteen, think about making this toast:

'To the sky, from whence it came;
To the earth, where it nourishes life.' "

July 30 -- We went out seton-watching. I had a really neat place. It was way down in the woods. I was out on a rock and there was -- I don't know what it was, but it was off in the bushes rattling around and then it ran away. I thought that was pretty neat. I never knew what it was. Someone else heard it, too, and they didn't know what it was, either. At first I thought -- it's a MOOSE!

SETON WATCHING. Sitting or standing in a place and freezing -- not rigidly, but in a relaxed way; totally stilling your body and opening yourself to the environment.

"We call this the Seton Journey because of Ernest Thompson Seton. He was a naturalist who roamed the wild spaces of Canada and the U.S. in the early 1900's. He would sit for hours just observing. The technique of 'seton-watching' is based on the way he would let nature come to him. He'd just sit and kind of immerse himself in the world around him.

"When you start, find a comfortable position, maybe sitting like this with your back resting against a tree and your legs stretched out; go over your entire body mentally -- do you feel pressure anywhere? Adjust your position . . . loosen . . . ease. Take a couple of deep breaths, let the air out very slowly, and settle into a state of motionlessness. If you will sit absolutely still like this, completely motionless, after fifteen minutes or so the natural world will begin to sweep over you as if you weren't even there. It will literally engulf you as the wild animals return to their normal patterns.

"I really enjoy seton-watching. When sitting silently, I find that my mind just flows along easily from one thing to another. And the natural world seems so real and so vivid that it sometimes fills me with an indescribable emotion. If you give it a chance and practice patience, seton-watching can be a lot of fun. Sometimes you'll see animals; sometimes you may just hear the wind and watch the trees. But whatever happens, somehow it's very special and very personal."

August 2 -- I have decided to be more frank with my log on the subject of my reflections. Here are some of the qualities that I feel I have gained or enhanced on the Seton Journey:

1. To respect the passage of time, but not to continually fret about it;

2. To be considerate of others by cleaning up after myself and by maintaining a low level of noise;

3. To respect (appreciate) our basic resources and necessities: water, sunlight, shelter, sleep, food, and fire;

4. To respect energy and stamina;

5. To truly appreciate the qualities of cordiality and understanding;

6. To respect the need for cooperation in all situations;

7. And mostly, to respect (appreciate) nature and wildlife by observation in its natural habitat, and that living with nature is not unrealistic but a necessary part of society.

SEEDS. Short meaningful quotations about life to focus our awareness on one thought.

"After our mid-morning or mid-afternoon break each day, I will give you two seeds. One will be like this -- an edible seed from one of these pouches to suck on as you hike. The other will be a seed to hold in your mind, a piece of wisdom to think about along the way. The seed in your mouth will help your body keep its balance of salt and water; the seed in your mind can grow into many thoughts.

"After the breaks, when it is time for receiving the seeds, you can get your packs ready to go. I'll go to each person in turn, offering him one of these seeds from the pouch and giving him the seed for his mind at the same time. This way, you'll all hear me repeating the words of the seed as I give it to each in turn. Hearing and watching the others receive the seeds will help plant them more deeply in your own mind.

"Let's get ready to move out, now. Here is your seed:

'You cannot do just one thing.'
'You cannot do just one thing.'
'You cannot do just one thing.'
'You cannot do just one thing.'

We were thinking about the sky. You never think about the sky as being there. We started thinking about the sky, though. It's like the sky is always there, no matter where you go. It's the same sky. The sky sees pine trees here and it sees the city. Every place you go, the sky keeps moving. It's a weird thought.

SKY. The atmosphere -- the cradle of clouds and stars, sun and moon, weather and moods.

"Sometimes when you're walking, just look up and sense the sky. Instead of looking ahead or around, or thinking about the weight or the destination or even the forest, just focus on the sky and consider it.

"As we lie here, looking at the sky, think about how important it is to life; from about two miles above us to one mile below us, the air makes life possible. The atmosphere -- the sky we see as a vast dome -- is so very thin between us and the cold lifelessness of space.

"The sky is kind of the playground -- the stage -- for the sun and moon and stars all in their turn. Since the beginning of time, man has looked out each morning at the sky, wondering at and trying to read its many moods. Man has often gazed at the stars and pondered the deep questions about life. The sky is also where we look to see the weather. We search the sky for the approach of weather and we try to predict it -- is it cloudy or clear? If it's a fine day, we usually feel good, too; the sky can help determine our moods.

"Or we see beauty in a sunrise or sunset, clouds against a backdrop of light. Like Emerson said, the sky really is 'the daily bread of the eyes,' the canopy, fathomless and deep. See it. Think about it."

We stopped for lunch on a big rock overlooking Chickenbone Lake. In a marsh to our left we heard a splash. A female moose climbed up out of the water and lumbered onto shore. Suddenly I felt I was really out in the wilderness, secluded from civilization, alone with the moose.

WANDERING. The nomadic life; not knowing what's around the next bend; movement from place to place, day by day, with no permanent home.

"The ancient peoples of the earth were probably nomadic. They had to roam to find suitable food, such as game animals or edible plants. Even today, for many people, roaming and being constantly on the move is a way of life. The Seton Journey is this way. Though it is only a brief taste of the nomadic life, it introduces you to some of the joys and limitations of that style.

"This footprint in the earth is almost symbolic of the Seton Journey. Perhaps you will never walk this way again, putting your feet where you are putting them now. That's one reason we don't concentrate on a destination. Once we reach the end of this trail, the journey will be over. We are on a journey, not to get there, but to be HERE, to be alert each day to the newness of what we pass.

"In our wanderings we can explore a lot of new things. It's an adventure to be seeing new places every day. Each day is unexpected, unplanned and surprising in its freshness.

"But there are limitations. A bad storm can be a near disaster because we have no stable place and no secure roof and walls. The people we meet will pass on by, so there are only transitory relationships. And we're never really settled in anywhere.

"So it is a journey, giving us a small dose of the wandering life. You may want to think about how you like to live, what degrees of wandering-settledness feel good to you; for both styles have their merits. The Seton Journey is ten days of wandering."

We need to keep the moose, the wolves, the birds and squirrels. They really are beautiful. Not maybe in looks as we usually think of beautiful, but as things that exist. The sheer fact that man has tried to dispose of such animals for his own self-esteem or through ignorance is really appalling! I only hope this program can stay for a long while; the Seton Journey can continue to show boys who turn into men what nature is all about. So he can't say to his children: "When I was a boy we HAD things called moose, wolves, birds, squirrels, etc., etc." If we can enlighten more people . . . we can keep the beautiful things we have.

READINGS. Special passages taken from the writings of our naturalists.

"One of the primary reasons for the Seton Journey is natural observation. This leather folder has some selections from the writings of other people who have observed the natural world before us. I'll read some every night, by the light of this candle stub. The candle will illuminate our awareness in lighting the words of the naturalists.

"The readings are for many reasons: to hear what has been said by others who have done what you are going to do, and to learn something about their styles and personalities. The readings may also deepen your experiences as you try to become more aware of this world of nature, and the words of these people may help broaden your horizons and give you new perspectives.

"We'll sit down each evening at dusk around a small fire, just before settling in for the night. Just as the seeds give you something to think about as you hike, perhaps the readings will give you something to dream about as you rest.

"This evening I would like to begin with a selection from Ernest Thompson Seton's *Wild Animals I Have Known*. . . ."

August 3 -- During the night I woke up five times, and every time I got up I looked at the sky because the whole sky was full of stars. We were alone with the stars because without all the city lights the whole sky was just illuminated. I've never seen them in an area where it was that dark, and they showed out like that. I don't know, but you'd think that around one of those there must be life. That's what is really neat about it -- thinking about stuff like that. I could~have stayed out longer.

EVENING RITUAL. Spending a few minutes alone in the evening, reviewing the day, taking time out to be silent.

"Our evening ritual is as simple as the morning ritual, and it can help us end our day with the same magic with which it began. Essentially, it is taking time in the evening to be alone with yourself, thinking through the day. We eat together, hike together, play together -- are together most of the day. The evening is a time to be alone and to reflect. We'll separate -- each one to a private place -- and there return to ourselves to consider the meaning of all we've seen and done.

"Think about the day and maybe tune in and mull over some of the thoughts you've had on the trail. Or you can just sit and watch the night and look for the animal life that emerges at dusk. It's your time to be alone, basically, and your time to reflect. And it's a silent time."

Ernest Thompson Seton was a naturalist, an artist, and a student of Indian Lore. He travelled widely throughout the U.S. and Canada in the early 1900's observing the wildlife, making sketches, and writing his impressions. These notes became books like *Wild Animals I Have Known* and *Lives of the Hunted;* books intimately describing the free open life of wild creatures. Seton was a great observer of nature. He could sit motionless for long periods of time just watching the natural world and becoming part of it. Because of his dedication to wildlife, his love for the land and its creatures, and his loose, easy style of roaming and observing in the wild, we chose to create a "Seton Journey" as part of our tripping program.

The Seton Journey is an in-depth experience in natural awareness and brings heightened enjoyment of the natural world. This is a central goal. It also aims to strengthen bodies, refresh minds, and open hearts. And, of course, we have a good time.

In a way, the journey is a study in paradoxes: feeling at home, yet being constantly on the move; feeling light and free, yet carrying a twenty-pound pack; being self-reliant, yet deeply aware of the need to help each other out. Perhaps these contradictions can be reconciled by the realization that they are not at all mutually exclusive, but rather may complement and enrich each other.

The Seton Journey is a life-style that is rarely lived anymore. Modern people have become very comfortable and very settled in this century, and it is our belief that a good way to both wake up from the tempting somnambulism of modern life AND yet appreciate its very real value and achievements is to experience a Seton Journey.

We live out in the woods, pitching wilderness camps and carrying our water. We hike, using our bodies and senses to the fullest. And we live wholesomely and simply with no paraphernalia. All this is somewhat like climbing a mountain or visiting a foreign country: it gives one a new perspective on life.

An individual may come back from a Seton Journey with an increased appreciation for running water, clean clothes, and prepared meals. But one may also experience pricks of disquietude about laziness and getting soft, and start wondering how to have the fun and adventure of Seton here in civilization. Then the journey has been a success -- something has been brought back -- and a young person starts thinking about improving the quality of his life by including the sparkle he has seen on Seton.

general

- leadership is crucial -- the leader must really be "tuned in" to the inputs. Sincerity cannot be faked, and there is no substitute for involvement.

- do not overload; excessively heavy packs detract from both the pleasure and purpose of the journey -- if necessary, cache food ahead of time.

- do have shakedowns previous to the journey; hike with loaded packs for an afternoon or more.

- check packs before leaving: what's on the list goes, what isn't stays behind!

- capitalize on opportunities to reinforce the inputs; you're building the concept with each occasion. Every input for the Seton Journey is relevant to the activities of almost every day -- when the campers start pointing out pace, rhythms, or the sky, you'll know the concepts are developing!

cooperation

- they've heard sermons on cooperation before. Make this REAL.

- we hold hands while sitting, and then stand up together to emphasize our interdependence, our need for cooperation.

natural observation

- take time at least once a day for natural observation. The timing is flexible, and the leader should take advantage of special opportunities: following a moose, for example. Or have some of the natural observation time in the early morning -- do it at different times of day.

- take off the packs!

- for the input, have the group sit in a circle. Then, have them face out so each makes a natural observation to share with the group.

log

- have prepared in advance the notebooks for use as logs; each has an oil-cloth pouch to carry the writing pad and a pencil.

- give the campers an opportunity to see samples of logs -- from explorers and naturalists and last year's Seton Journeyers -- perhaps before leaving camp or enroute to the site (e.g., the boat to Isle Royale).

- some suggestions for pre-entries in the prepared logs:

    -- a column ruled in to enter the day and date, perhaps the time, of the notation.
    -- a calendar of the days of the trip.
    -- an excerpt from one of Seton's own logs, or that of another naturalist or explorer.

●set aside special times for making entries in the logs: every day after the noon meal might be one good time; and the logs should be used during the daily natural observation time.

walking

●form the circle for this input with the path running through the diameter of the circle -- so choose a section of the trail that is open enough to allow getting off the path.

●there are many excellent books about the mechanics and the joys of walking. There are also some mediocre books about walking. Some of the good books include the following:

> The Complete Walker
> Home In Your Pack
> Backpacking: One Step at a Time

●one hikers' tip that is often stressed, seldom followed, and therefore worth reemphasizing, is the simple act of washing feet when water is available and then changing socks.

morning ritual

●see the guidelines for the *soft tool* in the chapter on Crusoe Camp.

●be sure that people spread out for the morning ritual, so each can enjoy silence, solitude.

●this is just a pre-breakfast wash-up -- after breakfast, there is tooth-brushing, using baking soda from a small pouch for the cleaning agent.

●the morning ritual is a good example of the importance of attitude: the same actions could be considered mundane and routine; but add a sparkle to it -- magic -- and washing one's face becomes a way of increasing awareness! The simplest actions of daily life can be charged with joy.

●soap is not allowed in the waters of Isle Royale; it isn't essential, anyway, and is probably best omitted from most water resources!

rhythms

●the Seton Journey basically has a dawn to dusk schedule. There may be times when dawn comes too early for the rhythms of a tired hiker's body, however. Pay attention to body rhythms as well as the rising and setting of the sun, but also note that a regular schedule of sleeping and rising is almost always beneficial!

●if the input on rhythms follows a period of rest, do a little exercise to help focus on the heart beat.

●as with most of the inputs, the leader should take advantage of the many opportunities to reemphasize rhythms -- at mealtimes, getting up, and going to bed. Assimilation is an important part of any learning process.

●there are rhythms in the mind as well as in the body, times when one feels alert and happy and times when one feels contemplative or like day-dreaming. These, too, are natural rhythms, not abnormalities to be worried about. Sharing this with young people may help them understand their moods.

simplicity   ●have specific packing instructions for the trip, listing what goes in the pack, down to the last item. Everyone has everything on the list -- and nothing else. No flashlights, radios, sheath knives, or yo-yo's!

**care for
yourself**   ●there are many alternative focal points: the leader can mend something or repair a piece of gear, or if water is available, wash his feet.

●although each is responsible for caring for himself, the leader should keep things moving smoothly.

pace   ●there should be ten minutes per hour for rest breaks. If there is to be an input, circle up at the END of the regular break.

energy   ●for the focal point here, pass out pieces of candy to suck on. Use individual pieces or a candy bar that can be broken into enough pieces for each to have one.

water   ●this is an activity in which the leader sets the tone by performing the "toast." He raises the canteen "to the sky from whence it came," then pours out one drop "to the earth, where it nourishes life," and then drinks himself. The others may adopt the ritual on their own.

**seton-
watching**   ●seton-watch for at least twenty minutes at a time, and at least once a day. Do it when the opportunity arises, and try various times of day.

●be sure people are spread out so that no one can see anyone else, no one can see the trail, and no one can be seen from the trail. Spread them out in their positions and re-group by coming back to pick them up.

●insects can be a problem during seton-watching. Consider a good insect repellant, but use it cautiously, for the odor intrudes upon the natural environment; you're more noticeable. If the insects are really bad, think about trying mosquito netting.

seeds

- prepare small leather pouches ahead of time. Each, when filled, can be held comfortably in one hand. We made ours from a leather chamois, running a leather thong through slits in the upper edges.

- use seeds with husks, so they can be sucked on for a long time. Large seeds are best. And salt the husks, to add that needed mineral for the body's balance of salt and water (suggested seeds: sunflower, squash, pumpkin).

- have the seeds once a day -- a thought and a seed.

sky

- have everyone in the circle turn around and lie down on their backs like "spokes of a wheel," heads in the center, eyes toward the sky.

wandering

- play down the destination -- emphasize the here and now.

readings

- we select our readings from the following books:

  Walden, Henry David Thoreau
  Journey Into Summer, Edwin Way Teale
  A Sand County Almanac, Aldo Leopold
  The Yosemite, John Muir
  The Sea Around Us, Rachel Carson
  Red Salmon, Brown Bear, T. J. Walker
  One Day on Beetle Rock, Sally Carrighar
  Wild Animals I Have Known, Ernest Thompson Seton
  The Wilderness Sampler, Jean Vermes
  Our Natural World, Hal Borland

- the campfire is very, very small -- like at Crusoe, just large enough so that all can huddle around it. The candle is essential because the tiny fire does not cast enough light. The stub is stuck on a log -- besides being useful, it's also kind of neat!

- have thick, short pieces of wood with which to feed the fire -- not much wood, heat, nor light is required.

evening ritual

- this input comes after the readings, to close the campfire. From there, each goes off separately for his evening ritual.

205

WALDEN SOLO

I do not feel lonely out here. I feel more the sense of being alone . . . or just having myself as company.

Most of the night was cloudless, and the sky was full of stars. I could see the Milky Way and have no idea of what else was beyond. The whole background of faint, pinprick stars was visible.

Everything seems to come together. The beauty of this place is poetic. It's like a gigantic, interwoven poem, and I can stick strands of it in and onto paper.

The whole day has been delicately overcast. Occasionally a few meagre drops of rain fell, but not for long. There's been a lot of things I've been thinking about while I've been walking.

The Walden Solo is being alone in the wilderness. From the first evening until noon on the third day, there is solitude. Each of the six teen-agers is alone and on his own, with the leader only passing by to see that each is well. With the solitude comes a special kind of freedom -- to think, to feel, and to be as one wishes. In his own place, half of a mile square in area, the young person can explore and contemplate and absorb the workings of nature.

With the advantages of solitude and self-reliance come the challenges of being responsible for one's own needs and of structuring one's own time. This solo experience does not, however, pit the individual AGAINST the environment. It is not a test of strength nor of ability to survive in the woods. Rather, the emphasis is on the qualities of awareness, identity, individuality, self-expression, contemplation, and harmony -- becoming one with nature, flowing easily and living simply and honestly within the environment. For man IS a part of nature; pitting himself against his environment is but an act of egotistical folly. Man can never really "overcome" nature, because he cannot overcome himself. Far better that he seek his rightful place within the harmony, the ongoing life of the natural world.

True, the environment can be hostile to a human being who is unprepared, ill-quipped -- who does not know how to handle himself or does not have the skills to care for his basic needs. But in that sense, the environment is no more hostile to man than to any living thing. An amoeba "faces" the same requirements, yet man prides himself on the struggle! It is only because we view ourselves as something apart that we feel threatened.

The challenge that the Walden Solo makes to the individual is not a physical test. It is a challenge to BE, to become again a part of the environment and let the environment become a part of one's life. If there is a confrontation involved, it is not between man and nature, but between man and his sense of identity, a struggle with the deepest questions of existence. For this, the wilderness environment is a free and harmonious setting. Finding one's self and finding nature, become, in the end, the same search.

Walden is a place to stop talking for a while in order to listen -- to absorb. If you go into the wilderness, alone and quiet, to discover the nature of life, you may not find it. But if you give it a chance, it may find you.

Thoreau chose to go to Walden on July 4, 1845. Today, almost one hundred and thirty years later, I have come to the woods to recapture some of Thoreau's basic emotions . . . Today being the first day of my three-day stay, I shall try to set up some goals that will increase my self-awareness and help me to become one with nature itself. I wish to attempt to forget our society's values and simplify life to barest necessities. I believe that many of us are constantly burdened with superficial values. Like Thoreau, I do not wish to spend my life running after nothing.

NOTEBOOK. A record of the experiences of Walden Solo.

"Out there, without other people, without planned stimulation, without the props and diversions of society, I think your notebook is going to be important to you. It will probably become a very close friend in just a few days. You may spend a lot of time with this new friend, exploring feelings and thoughts you've never experienced before.

"You may meet loneliness or exhilaration or confusion or peacefulness, and it might feel good just to be able to share what's happening in some way. I really enjoy a notebook. Sometimes it's like talking to myself, clearly and without interruption. Sometimes I become more aware of the miracle of language and how it provides us with a way of expressing ourselves; yet other times discover its inadequacies when I'm trying to put deep feelings and experiences into words.

"Anyway -- your notebook is your friend -- a valued companion for a solo experience."

The fact that I am really alone is just beginning to be realized in my mind. When I first turned back, the thought rushed through my mind that this is it -- I'm really alone. But it was quickly drowned. I think now that it is because I am not alone at all. I am surrounded by trees and moss and water and rocks and birds and flowers and nature. The only way that it can seem more lonely than the massive, cold, impersonal cities of man is in its strangeness. And it does not seem strange out here -- it seems familiar, and warm. The sunlight is glintering through the trees.

SOLITUDE. Being totally alone -- not dependent on anyone else for company, aid, or conversation.

"I think solitude is kind of the heart of the whole Walden Solo. You are going to spend three days alone -- with no one else. We'll pass by once or twice a day just to make sure everything is cool and you're all right, but we'll keep it short and nonverbal. Hopefully it will be as unobtrusive as possible so as not to interrupt the flow and feeling of your solitude.

"Being alone is maybe a little scary. Being alone in the woods (learning to be with yourself), using your own time, spending the night alone: all these are challenges. They're not big physical challenges; they're more subtle and mental, but challenges just the same.

"Solitude increases awareness, both natural awareness and self-awareness. Stop everything and just listen for a moment . . . Without words, without someone to talk to, all the natural sounds become more vivid and it is much easier to feel a part of nature. It takes some courage to turn your back on society's busy secure ways for a bit and go to the woods to be alone. Increased awareness is a fruit of this solitude. So also are peace, quiet, and tranquility."

*I'm sitting here, naked, looking down over the valley, writing this
... I have a sense of being purified. An urge has been satisfied and I'm
more at peace with myself. Being in nature by yourself brings out a
feeling that can be felt no where else. The feeling is freedom to do
what you want. The nature around you does something to your mind.
There is so much to learn from this beauty ... from the sticks, flowers,
and rocks on the ground.*

SENSING CIRCLE. Awakening senses to the beauties
of the natural environment.

"The solo experience is a chance for you to totally immerse yourself in the natural environment, without the distractions and diversions of society. To do this, you need to open up your senses -- un-
clog all the filters. Let's start by opening our mouths and noses and
taking in a big gulp of air and really smelling it ... Now, lie back, with
your feet in the center, and spread your arms out wide, so our circle
looks like the rays of the sun. With your outstretched arms, feel the
plants on the ground . . . Walk through them with your fingers . . .
Now, close your eyes, and listen to all the sounds around you. Don't
label them, just let them drift in and out of your consciousness . . .
Pick out one sound, now, and by concentrating on it, make it build
and die away . . . Weave the sounds in and out like the music of a
symphony orchestra.

"With your eyes still closed, roll over onto your stomach. Hug the
earth; 'grok' the ground. . . Feel it with your face and your hands and
your body . . . Smell it. Maybe taste it; taste what's growing from it.
And with your face right up against it, open your eyes and look at the
earth.

"Now lie quietly for a moment and bring all the elements
together: the sights, sounds, tastes, smells, and textures of this place
. . . Add the new dimensions to the symphony -- orchestrate all the
parts that make up your awareness. . . Put them together and let them
take over. Listen -- with all your senses, now -- to the orchestra. . ."

What are the purposes of times, clocks, and watches? For convenience? I can see how they would be useful in meeting a person, but man has over-used these times. For instance, meals are always eaten at a certain time. While I have been out here, I have had no way to judge time. I just eat when I'm hungry and drink when I'm dry. Pretty soon, I will go to eat dinner.

INDEPENDENCE. Being responsible for taking care of your own needs.

"Being independent is, for the Walden Solo, being able to get along WITHOUT others. You decide when to cook your meals -- and you cook them. You rig your own shelter -- and you sleep in it. You are responsible for keeping a supply of firewood dry, keeping your gear under cover, and generally taking care of yourself.

"This independence is an important part of growing into adulthood. Probably from now on in your lives you will have an increasing amount of independence and with this independence an added responsibility for yourself and perhaps later for others. So experiencing independence, learning to take the time and effort to care for yourself and your belongings, is rather vital to your healthy growth as a person.

"And maybe one of the best ways is to face this directly, to realize that out here no one else will care for you and you have to do it. It's not a drag. Actually, it's kind of fun, this setting up a little home in the natural world, this independence.

"There are a couple of limits. First, because you will be alone, stick within a quarter mile of your shelter -- explore your own area. And if you happen to run across anyone else, communicate nonverbally -- or maybe not at all. Tonight, when we meet here for the final time, take your place in the circle silently, so we'll have nonverbal communication until after the next input. This way, we won't disturb each other's independence."

*Last night, before I went to sleep, I put my candle out and lit it.
Before long, there was a moth that came and circled the candle. I
asked myself, why is this moth attracted to my candle? Not from the
heat, I'm sure. After a while, I blew the candle out. The moth was
gone. It seemed to me that the moth was much like man. Man is often
attracted to things that won't benefit him in any way.*

> FLOW. Minutes and hours dissolve into the raw facts
> of experience and being.

"Look at the clouds.

"One of the most incredible things that happens on the Solo is
that you feel the lack of time structuring. When you are out here
without schedules or watches or clocks, somehow time becomes
meaningless and in its place there is only flow. Instead of eating at
8:00 every morning, you eat when you get up and get hungry and fix
something. And then there is just kind of raw time to fill with experiences. All your life and consciousness seems to melt from a
structured, ordered pattern into a flow of experiences determined not
by what time it is, but by how you feel and what you want and need.
And it's kind of neat."

"Listen to the stream.

"Flowing, like solitude, increases awareness. If you're not
worried about time, you are freed up to put all of yourself into experiencing. And since there are no time pressures, you are free to explore things to their depths: a tree, the sky, yourself. Life is richer
when you are flowing along from experience to experience. The only
guides to time out here are night and day. Minutes and hours dissolve
into the raw facts of being."

Life is what one makes it. I really feel that this is true. It may be harder for one person to enjoy life than others, but if everyone worked hard and took steps in the right direction, life could become much more liveable. But often, people take steps in the wrong direction. For instance, take the person who is always after money. No matter how much he can get, no matter how rich, money cannot make him happy. Many people pursue false values, such as money -- I among them, I suppose. So to make life better, I should pursue the more meaningful things in life.

> INDIVIDUALITY. Being yourself; getting away from artificial or untrue ways of relating and being.

"You are an individual, different from any other person on earth. You are free to be yourself here. There is no competition, no need to impress or convince anyone. The only requirement -- if there is one at all -- is to BE. Hopefully, in this atmosphere you will begin to discover your own individual style. Thoreau said, 'If a man does not keep pace with his companions, perhaps it is because he hears the beat of a different drummer. Let him step to the music he hears, however measured or far away.'

"The nuts in this basket are all different -- each has a shell, and each shell opens to reveal the seed inside. They come from different places; they would grow into different plants. They are the same in many ways -- and different in many others. You are like that, too.

"There are enormous pressures on us to conform to some kind of norm during our lives. Of course, we cannot be totally undisciplined and disregardful of others. That would be wrong. But we can nonetheless avoid being a person who is alive only to please others. We can grow to know that special thing we are -- our uniqueness as persons -- our individuality. Here on the Walden Solo -- and ever after -- be yourself."

Before I continue writing in my journal, I must verify one thing. What I write is only now, how I feel at a certain time, nothing more. If I write something today, it does not mean I will agree with it tomorrow.

> *solitude is like*
> *a young tree in the meadow*
> *beautiful and clear*

PERSPECTIVE. Seeing your whole life from a new vantage point; stepping back and reflecting on direction, values, needs, feelings.

"The Walden Solo is a chance to get a new perspective on your life. It's a kind of retreat, a time when you can think about your most basic goals and then, perhaps, change them or act upon them. By being away, by casting aside the unessentials and confronting the basic facts of life, and by a deeper knowing of yourself, you can come to a new awareness of your life in society. Thoreau went to the woods to live and enjoy nature, but he also went to get a new perspective on the mass of men and what they were doing. He found in solitude a sublime peace that life 'in the world' could not offer. He also discovered that 'a man is rich in proportion to the number of things he can afford to let alone.'

"The Solo may make you think about the things you do back home. Some of your activities are important and meaningful; some may seem unimportant and meaningless. You might decide to spend more time alone, even plan to get out and walk by yourself. You may glimpse some feelings and joys that you were unaware of and wonder if it is possible to sustain them. The Solo is a chance to evaluate and to think through what is really important to you. What are the things that really matter?

"Think about some part of your self that you are beginning to see from a new perspective. Let the stick you have brought to our campfire symbolize something you want to illuminate. It's an 'awareness' stick because the light of its fire will help you see yourself. Place the stick, silently, on our fire."

In the next few pages, I shall tell about each sense and what I'm sensing at the time. . .

Hearing. Right now, I am listening to the river and rain. Occasionally I hear a bird singing in the distance. Unlike taste, I think there are times when you never hear anything. But these times are short, and seldom. In fact, I think we are almost always hearing something. What fascinating and amazing things are our bodies! For instance, our hearts are always beating; we are always breathing. We do all these things all of our life, 'til finally we die. Sometimes, for some people, this goes on for a hundred years!

COMTEMPLATION. The ability to receive the world in a passive way.

"One of the central aspects of the Walden Solo is contemplation. Thoreau says in his book that he could, and often did, just sit on his doorstep from morning to noon, totally absorbed in what was happening in the woods. He didn't need to move or jump about or distract himself with 'Well, I've got to find something to do!' He was content to sit and receive what the natural world said to him.

"We are not used to contemplating in our culture. Genuinely contemplating requires persistent, full attention and quite a bit of patience. Here are two guidelines:

1. Be silent -- not only by not talking, but by not using words. Get behind the words. Try for a while to perceive without labeling.
2. Don't try too hard. Don't try to think profound thoughts. Just sit and watch nature and let things flow through you. Don't try to make them go anywhere. Follow them. Receive.

"The solo is a good opportunity to learn the art of contemplation in its fuller sense. If you still yourself, if you take time to really look and see and feel what is in the natural world and not just run around in it, you will begin to enjoy one of the greatest pleasures man can ever experience -- contemplation."

I have been thinking here, alone, on top of a great moss-covered rock. I have just been inspired about one of the great values of the Solo: getting to know one's self. Out here, we are stripped of everything but one's self. You cannot help but learn more about what you really are. You can be yourself without worrying about interactions with anyone else. Out here, you have to be yourself -- there is no one else to be. There are no cars, no houses, no time, no schools, no people to interfere with your own mind. There is only nature. Only things which have been here for centuries. Things which belong here.

IDENTITY. Discovering "the me that is me."

"Here is a quote from Thoreau's, *Walden,* for you to think about:

Not till we are lost, in other words not till we have lost the world, do we begin to find ourselves, and realize where we are and the infinite extent of our relations.

"This is a call to self-awareness -- to discovering your own identity. In the solitude of the Walden Solo, you will be very aware of your own SELF -- your body and how it feels; your thoughts and how they roam. This is a chance to probe a little into the questions, 'Who am I?' and 'What is my place in the world?' It's a good chance to leave behind the standard identifications you have in society -- school or friends or grades or sports or car -- and get away from expectations and roles to discover your real naked self behind all these. We have an essential self, a real identity if we but take the time to listen to ourselves and our deepest feelings and thoughts. And I think you'll find this a very positive -- a very real -- and a very exhilarating experience."

My new vantage point is back on the creek. I'm sitting on a-rock that is covered with moss. The rock is sitting in a deeper part of the stream. The patterns which the rock is making on the flowing parts of the water are endless. They are always changing. The water will never come back to touch the rock. The light shining on the water seems to make it white in some spots. The lines that are white scatter about the surface.

HARMONY. Living in agreement and accord with the natural world.

"Out here, without pressures, without schedules, without being told what to do, you may have this nice mellow feeling come up inside you. Though there's really no word that ever quite fits this feeling, we'll just call it 'harmony' so we can talk about it for a bit.

"Harmony is a state of non-striving -- non-needing -- non-wanting. It means getting along easily, without stress or strain or disruption or destruction; this goes for getting along with yourself, with others, and with nature. Most of our lives are spent doing something to gain a certain end. Out here you can be freed up from some of that and, if you lay back and let it happen, harmony may just slip into your mind -- into you. It may seem that all the plants and all the trees and the whole sky are smiling at you benevolently.

Or you may wake up knowing you can do whatever you want that day. And you may find yourself with a good feeling about the day and thinking that this is the way life should be -- the way you and life were meant to be."

It is raining now. Not hard, but a determined drizzle. The rain seems to purify everything. It cleans the air and the wood. Walking through the rain is a far-out experience. Instead of ducking into the nearest shelter, as in civilization, I am free to experience the rain. It is rare for me, or anyone in civilization, to actually be out in the rain, except when scurrying for shelter. It is just great to sit and watch it rain on you. It's great just to sit and listen.

AFTERTHOUGHT. A commitment to carry Walden back.

"On the Walden Solo, you've been asked to think about your values -- the things that are really important to you. But if you really hold a value, you must be willing to act on it; if you don't do anything about it, you probably don't hold it as a value at all. It's one thing to be out here and have this experience and think about how you want your life to be. But you can go back to the city and to the same lifestyle -- the same activities and values -- you had before."

"So now, while you're still here, make a commitment to yourself to DO something about the values you think you hold about this experience. Right now, print the word 'Afterthoughts' in capital letters at the top of the last page of your notebook. Make a promise to yourself -- a commitment -- to return to the notebook on a specific date. It may be one or two or ten days from now; but on that day, come back to the notebook, spend some time reading and thinking it over, and write your afterthoughts. See if you still agree with what you have written, or if you have changed your mind or even gone beyond. Think about your values -- and then act on them."

Many of the goals of the Walden Solo are similar to those of the other trips: increasing natural awareness, living harmoniously, gaining a new perspective on life, slowing down and getting in touch with some basic facts about ourselves. However, with its emphasis on introspection and contemplation, the Solo is probably the deepest of the four. Walden Solo is an encounter with yourself in the natural world.

We hope the boys, by being alone for three days, will really begin to clarify some of their thinking. Without the big rush and the over-stimulation that sometimes takes control of modern life, there is time for thoughts to grow and mature -- like seeds in moist soil and sunlight. Heightened awareness of the natural environment -- and, thus, heightened enjoyment is another fruit of solitude. We believe that this increase in environmental perception-pleasure will result in greater attention to environmental values.

The uncovering of identity and the emergence of individuality help clarify social values as well. Should I go to college or not? Should I become a biologist or a writer? Is this relationship with this person meaningful, or are we just making out? These kinds of questions need time to be thought out carefully in an undisturbed atmosphere. Young people in our culture rarely get the chance to think deeply, and if they do, often don't know how to handle it.

The Solo is an attempt to give them this opportunity. Larger social values are important too. Thoreau thought about them all -- and we encourage young people to do the same.

Seclusion in a wilderness setting offers the opportunity to examine one's usual life-style and surroundings from a more detached perspective. But the Walden Solo is more than just a vantage point for thinking about other places; it has much to offer in its own right. How strange that we so often think about being somewhere else -- and then when we are there, dream of being back here. The Solo does help clarify thoughts concerning the "there" -- by unclogging perceptual filters, removing the blinders of habit, and clearing out partitions that tend to pigeonhole thought. In solitude -- in nature -- one can think and feel more clearly on the subject of his contemplations, be it himself, his society, or his natural environment.

In addition to values clarification, a major thrust of the Walden Solo is an experience with the non-verbal skills of receptivity, openness, and silence. These are other neglected areas in our culture. Young people need to learn to see things with their own eyes; they need to know how to be quiet and passively enjoy a sunset or a tree or a flower. They need to know there are wide worlds of perception and emotion that language cannot begin to describe.

The Solo helps them know these worlds and simultaneously makes them aware of the fact that, although words fall far short, it IS nice to have words. It is nice to be able to communicate at all, because on the Solo another thing that happens is that one really begins to appreciate other people. And maybe one is a little kinder -- a little more considerate and thoughtful -- upon returning.

Walden Solo is an experience in what it means to be a human being.

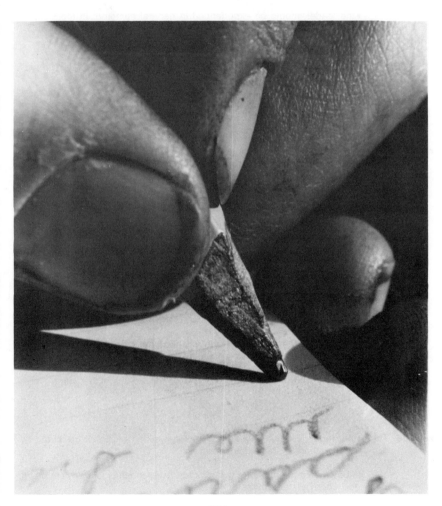

general
- have a preparation meeting with the people who will be going on the Solo. This is a time when they can work on making the journals and go over the mechanics of the trip.

- packing list: make it clear that THIS is IT (i.e., no transistor radios or other extras).

- explain briefly how it will go: the first day is going in, some inputs, setting up, silent time alone, a re-grouping for evening campfire, then a night and a day and a night of solitude.

- the Walden Solo is for ages 14 and older. Participants should have previous experience in camping, perhaps in backpacking, too. They should have stable and mature personalities.

- the leader should be experienced in general camping: in most cases, getting to a wilderness site will require some backpacking.

- the leader should be experienced in basic first aid. Take a good first aid kit along and provide each camper with a supply of necessary first aid materials.

- the only watch that goes along is the one used by the leader.

notebook
- this input is given at the preliminary meeting, with the group in a circle, and a sample notebook as the focal point.

- we make our own notebooks, using natural materials: hand-spun virgin lamb's wool for the stitching; leather for the covers; medium weight grey construction paper and rice paper for the pages. (The boys spend some time preparing the notebooks at the preliminary meeting.) There are less elaborate alternatives that others might want to consider, but it is important that the journals be neat -- attractive -- special. Commercial notebooks can be purchased and re-covered.

- some of the later inputs for the Walden Solo are inserted in the notebook. The leaders can bind these into the "home made" editions, or paste them in the store-bought variety. We used calligraphy; neat printing, or typing could be substituted.

- personalize the books by inscribing the camper's name. We included some block prints as an added touch.

- give the notebooks out at the end of the first-night campfire.

solitude
- this input is done on the way to the Walden site. Form a circle by holding hands and sitting down.

- stop and listen; pause for two minutes. The tendency is always to go on too soon. Listen yourself! Wait.

•make it clear that when you pass by their places, you won't be "checking up" on them. When you go to their places, be discreet, quiet, non-verbal; you're there to give attention to the soloist's mental and physical well being. Just knowing someone is around in case of emergency does provide security.

sensing circle ·

•do this one on the way to the site after walking some distance from the previous input.

•if it's a warm day, suggest they remove shoes and socks, loosen belts and collars, perhaps take off their shirts. . .

•do the exercises slowly, at least twice as slowly as you think they should go!

independence

•if there's water around, include in the policies that there's to be no swimming alone. A person may want to sit in the water and take a "bird bath."

•the boundaries are partially for safety reasons, and partly because the whole point of Walden is not exploring far and wide, but exploring close to home.

flow

•give soloists about a half an hour to set up their shelters. Make the rounds, stopping at each site to give the "flow" input on a one to one basis and to make sure everything is going to be comfortable. Reemphasize the boundaries and safety precautions, and explain again that when returning for the campfire, the soloist should remain silent and take a seat and wait until the leader opens up the dialogue. Set up the "sun time" for coming in -- e.g., "when the sun touches the tip of that pine tree."

individuality

•have a small basket, empty, in the center of the circle. As people drift in, indicate a place for them to sit. They should remain silent until all are gathered. Then begin the input.

•buy seven different kinds of nuts, in shells: walnut, hickory, almond, filbert, brazil nut, pecan, pistachio, etc. Put them in a pouch. As you speak, transfer them, one by one, from the pouch to the basket.

•after the input, the nuts can be cracked with a rock and eaten.

•remind them of the Gestalt motto: "I am not in this world to live up to your expectations, and you are not in this world to live up to mine. You are you, and I am I."

• following this input, move away from the circle to a place with a good view of the sunset. Bring out extra nuts for a snack. Watch the sunset together. There can be quiet talking -- the word is "low-key." After the sun has set -- or after about an hour -- have them return to their places in the circle. Ask that each bring a small "awareness" stick with him for your fire.

perspective

• while the campers are finding their "awareness" sticks, build a small fire -- large enough for all to sit around, but no larger.

• each person adds his stick to the fire silently after thinking about it for a while. The symbolism should remain secret, an individual and a private decision. After the instruction to place the stick in the fire, be silent, giving time for thought.

• at the close of this, give them the Walden Notebooks and resume non-verbal communication as they return to their sites.

contemplation

• insert this input into the notebooks ahead of time.

identity

• this input is written in the notebook in advance.

• a picture of a stylized tree, with large leaves, might also be included in the notebook, with instructions to write or symbolize on each of the leaves some element that helps make up "the me that is me."

harmony

• this input is written on a piece of paper, folded in an unusual but simple way, and left at the soloist's site -- weighted down by a peach!

• the leader should try to remain unseen without making it into a game. As always when passing near the sites, he should be as unobtrusive as possible.

afterthoughts

• Pass by and pick the soloists up on the last day. Keep it non-verbal until back at the base camp or even the point where you hit the trail that leads back to civilization. Then stop for this input. Give them a chance to share some of their feelings about the Solo (see Crusoe Camp -- magic circle campfire).

• prepare for re-entry. At some point, a group swim might be in order. But the main adjustment to be made will probably be mental -- from the solitude to the hustle and bustle. Prepare them for this; maybe include it in the "rap." They may even bring it up first!

• BE SURE all litter, paper, garbage, etc., is packed out.

224

●the importance of the solo experience lies as much in what transfers as in what happens. Remember Thoreau: "I left the woods for as good a reason as I went there."